MADRID

CITYSCOPES: a unique overview of a city's past as well as a focused eye on its present. Written by authors with intimate knowledge of the cities, each book provides a historical account with essays on the city today. Together these offer fascinating vignettes on the quintessential and the quirky, the old and the new. Illustrated throughout with compelling historical images as well as contemporary photos, these are essential cultural companions to the world's greatest cities.

Titles in the series:

Beijing Linda Jaivin

Berlin Joseph Pearson

Buenos Aires Jason Wilson

Chicago: From Vision to Metropolis Whet Moser

London: City of Cities Phil Baker

Madrid: Midnight City Helen Crisp and Jules Stewart

Mexico City: Cradle of Empires Nick Caistor

New York Elizabeth L. Bradley

Paris Adam Roberts

Prague: Crossroads of Europe Derek Sayer

San Francisco: Instant City, Promised Land Michael Johns

CITYSCOPES

Madrid

Midnight City

Helen Crisp and
Jules Stewart

REAKTION BOOKS

To Michael, William and John

Published by Reaktion Books Ltd
Unit 32, Waterside
44–48 Wharf Road
London N1 7UX, UK
www.reaktionbooks.co.uk

First published 2020
Copyright © Helen Crisp and Jules Stewart 2020

Printed and bound in China by 1010 Printing International Ltd

A catalogue record for this book is available from the British Library
ISBN 978 1 78914 219 8

OPENING IMAGES p. 7: Calle del Toledo next to the Plaza Mayor; p. 8: Baroque façade of the
church of San Miguel, Calle de San Justo; p. 9: View down the Calle del Acuerdo towards
the Gran Vía; p. 10 Interior of bar 'El Anciano Rey de los Vinos' founded 1909; p. 11 (top):
Pinchos in the Mercado de San Miguel; p. 11 (foot): Table at the iconic Café Gijón; p. 12: Fans
for sale near the Plaza Mayor; p. 13: Balconies looking out onto the Plaza de Santa Ana;
p. 14: Carrión Building at Plaza del Callao; p. 15 (top): The Royal Palace; p. 15 (foot): The
Almudena Cathedral; p. 21: Plaza Mayor, mid-19th century; p. 147: Ginkgo Sky bar in the
Plaza de España; p. 102 Cafe tables on the Calle del Nuncio.

Contents

View of Madrid at twilight.

Prologue

On a balmy mid-May morning in 1561, King Felipe II of Spain climbed into his royal carriage in Toledo to embark on a historic 80-kilometre (50-mi.) journey northward across the Castilian plateau. The dour, black doublet-attired monarch's destination was an undistinguished township of some 9,000 inhabitants known as Magerit, derived from the Arabic طيرجم (Majrit), meaning 'the place of abundant water'. The name itself may offer a clue as to why Felipe decided to shift his capital to what would become Madrid.

For centuries before Francisco de Goya painted scenes of merrymakers dancing on the banks of the Manzanares, Madrid's river had served as a source of water for the fortified settlement. In Toledo, on the other hand, the daily chore of drawing water from the deep gorge of the Tagus for the city's thousands of court officials and bureaucrats, not to overlook the native population, was becoming too laborious a task. Parts of the Manzanares are now a haven for landlocked pleasure-seekers, with an artificial beach and riverside cafés, where Madrileños flock to escape the summer heat. It must not be forgotten that in the seventeenth century, it was an easily accessible source of vital drinking water.

Felipe never issued a decree proclaiming Madrid the new capital of his kingdom, nor did the monarch give a reason for his decision. As ruler of an empire that spanned the globe, embracing huge tracts of land in South and Central America, part of Western Europe and territories in Africa and the Far East, he felt under no obligation to do so. He simply declared that the court was to up sticks and move itself to the new seat of government. Until the twentieth century, there was no document in existence declaring Madrid the official capital of Spain. This was enshrined in the Constitution of the Second Spanish Republic in 1931 and reaffirmed in 1978 under the first democratic government to take power after the death of dictator Francisco Franco.

The choice of Madrid still remains an enigma to historians, Spanish and foreign alike. Francisco José Gómez Fernández writes,

> It certainly came as a surprise. No one expected it. The most powerful monarch to reign in centuries, Felipe II, chose a small upland town, which did not even enjoy the denomination of a city, which until that time had not played a relevant part in the centuries-old history of the country.

Toledo was a cramped place, lacking in sanitation facilities and adequate food supplies and held under scrutiny by a Church that did not look kindly on the court's permissive lifestyle. The archbishop of Toledo, who was the head of the Spanish episcopate, exercised greater power over the citizenry than even the nobility. Living under the shadow of this ecclesiastical meddler was not to Felipe's liking. On the other hand, choosing to relocate to a city like Lisbon or Barcelona would have posed a political risk, in that Castile was the monarchy's military mainstay, as well as a rich source of food, with its great stocks of cattle and sheep. Another factor in favour of Madrid was that it was a single day's journey from the site of El Escorial Monastery, which Felipe planned to build in the hills north of the city. There was also a sentimental strand to this momentous episode. The king's third wife, Elisabeth de Valois, had a strong dislike of Toledo and implored her husband to find a home where she might live in the style to which she was accustomed, away from this backwater perched above the Tagus River. Elisabeth could take pride in her new abode in Madrid, a des res worthy of the eldest daughter of France's King Henry II, albeit scarcely up to the standards of the Fontainebleau splendour of her birth.

When the Moorish invaders took Madrid in the mid-ninth century, they built a watchtower on the western perimeter of their fortress to keep a lookout for Christian troops. Felipe II's father, the Holy Roman Emperor Charles V (Carlos I of Spain), supplanted the derelict Muslim citadel with a fortress that in time became a five-hundred-room palace known as El Alcázar. This was Spain's royal residence until 1734, when on Christmas Eve a smouldering curtain in a corridor went unnoticed. As fire spread throughout the palace, some five hundred art treasures and paintings by Rubens, Velázquez and other masters went up in smoke. It was by sheer good fortune that a footman spotted the flames threatening Velázquez's *Las Meninas*. On a fortuitous instinct, sensing the painting might be of some value, the servant hurled it from a window into the courtyard below.

Felipe II laid the groundwork for Madrid's development from a township into a city worthy of its status as the highest capital in Europe, rising 670 metres (2,200 ft) above sea level. Many great monuments were built during the Habsburg monarch's reign: the Royal Convent of Las Descalzas, with its priceless collection of works by Titian, Rubens and Brueghel the Elder; the beginnings of the now bustling Plaza Mayor; the Baroque House of the Seven Chimneys, which in the seventeenth century became the British Ambassador's official residence; and, towering above all others in size and grandeur, the El Escorial monastery, a testimony to Madrid's role as the focal point of the Christian world, second only to Rome. This is where Felipe, ever a patron of the arts, assembled the collection of paintings by Titian, El Greco and other Renaissance masters that was to become the core of the Prado Museum when it was founded more than 250 years later.

Madrid's rapid expansion drew in a flood of people from the provinces – craftsmen, fortune-seekers, ruffians and swashbucklers, all eager to savour the life of the imperial capital and, most of all, to partake in the building boom. By the time of Felipe's death in 1598, Madrid's population had soared nearly tenfold to some 80,000 inhabitants. Barely a handful of them could call themselves *gato* (cat), a title that could only be claimed by a third-generation Madrileño: the name is taken from the nimble soldier who scampered up the Moorish battlements to tear down the enemy banner in the eleventh-century battle that ousted the Muslims from Madrid.

The spirit of Madrid was aptly defined by the American novelist Ernest Hemingway, always an eager partaker of the city's culture of late-night revelry:

> To go to bed at night in Madrid marks you as a little queer. For a long time your friends will be a little uncomfortable about it. Nobody goes to bed in Madrid until they have killed the night. Appointments with a friend are habitually made for after midnight at the café.

Our book is the story of a vibrant, creative and energetic metropolis, one that inspires the pride and loyalty characteristic of a city of immigrants. It is scarcely surprising that Madrileños maintain an unshakeable confidence in the saying *De Madrid al Cielo, y allí, un agujerito para verlo*: 'From Madrid to Heaven, and from there, a peephole to observe it.'

HISTORY

Remains of the old Arab walls of Magerit with the Almudena Cathedral in the background.

1 *Magerit* Becomes Madrid

Madrid is a young city resting on a bedrock of history that stretches back to the Palaeolithic age. If you take an afternoon stroll along the banks of the Manzanares River, you will find Madrileños luxuriating with a gin and tonic on the city's new artificial beach, facing no greater danger to their well-being than sunburn. In prehistoric times, these pleasure-seekers would have had to confront rhinos, hippos and mammoths, who were unlikely to have taken kindly to humans intruding upon their habitat. A menacing pair of mammoth tusks on display at the San Isidro Museum in the Plaza de San Andrés speaks eloquently of the perils that lurked on this spot several hundred thousand years ago.

In the earliest days of the city's recorded history, Madrid pulled no cultural or economic weight in Hispania. In 139 BC, the Roman legions that swept across Carpetania, which included the region of Madrid, paid scant attention to this tiny settlement, setting their sights instead on ports like Cádiz, Seville or Barcelona, with their links to the major Mediterranean trading hubs. Madrid was insignificant compared with venerable centres of philosophy and poetry such as Córdoba, the city that was to give the world luminaries like Seneca (4 BC–AD 65) and Lucan (AD 39–65). In those days Madrid and its surrounding region was overshadowed by Complutum, which boasted 50,000 inhabitants. This Roman outpost 32 kilometres (20 mi.) to the east on the Castilian plateau was a seat of learning. In the nineteenth century its university was shifted to Madrid, becoming known as the Universidad Complutense. Today the town is known as Alcalá de Henares, the birthplace of Miguel de Cervantes (1547–1616).

When the Visigoth hordes overran most of Roman Hispania in the sixth century AD, they integrated Madrid into the kingdom of Toledo, though this brought about almost no change in the settlement's isolated and rural status. It was not until the ninth century that Madrid came to take on the look of a township in its own right, in effect a large fortified village encircled by a system of defensive walls with three principal gates of entry. The Moorish emir Mohammed I set up his military headquarters in what he called Magerit, an Arabic term for water as a giver of life. This position was to be his first line of defence against the Christian forces advancing from the north.

Once the Muslims had been ousted from Magerit, the monarchs of Castile took to journeying to the city between campaigns to enjoy its salubrious climate and hunt game in its well-stocked woodlands. This had its disadvantages for the people of Madrid. The arrival of the monarch with thousands of court followers in tow put a great demand on available lodgings. By a royal decree – *regalia de aposento*, or 'right of abode' – Madrileños were obliged to offer sleeping quarters for these visitors. The key proviso was a clause that referred to those 'in possession of adequate living space'. This presented Madrileños with a golden opportunity to put into practice their picaresque talents. In time, new one-storey houses were built, but with a second or even a third floor set back to render it invisible from the street. In this way people could plead a lack of space to accommodate these visitors in a style befitting their exalted station. The authorities were not long in unmasking the ruse. Surveyors were sent out to inspect these suspected 'houses of malice', as they were called. In La Latina district and other historic neighbourhoods, you can see seventeenth-century tiles on the stone facades of some houses, bearing the inscription *Visita de Manzana G* and the number of the house under inspection.

Overall Madrid played an unremarkable role in the Reconquest, but it could hardly be considered a nonentity. The city has the curious distinction of being the only one in Spain to have borne the title of an independent kingdom. In 1383, Juan I of Castile granted sanctuary to Leo V (known in Spain as León V), the deposed king

Casas de Malicia, 'houses of malice', in Calle de Montserrat, showing the windows of the 'hidden' top storeys.

of Armenia, who had recently been released on ransom after having been held captive by the Egyptian Mamelukes. The Spanish monarch bestowed on his fellow Christian the title of king of Madrid. He ruled the city, much to the annoyance of its feudal lords, for eight years. Little trace remains of León v's presence in Madrid, apart from a restaurant near the Plaza Mayor and a Spanish brandy, both of which bear his name. In more recent times Madrid has been the

Statue of Santa María de la Cabeza on the Puente de Toledo.

Santa María de la Cabeza

The curiously named Santa María de la Cabeza (Saint Mary of the Head) was the wife of Madrid's patron saint, San Isidro. After her death, she became known as María de la Cabeza, as the reliquary containing her head was believed to bring rain from heaven when taken in procession around an area experiencing drought. For this, she was traditionally revered by farm workers.

María Torribia was born in Guadalajara, northeast of Madrid, in the early twelfth century. Legends about San Isidro and Santa María include one about their baby son miraculously being saved from drowning in a well, by the water rising to bring him to the surface. In thanks María and Isidro took a vow of celibacy, but sadly the child died in infancy, so there are no descendants of the holy pair.

She is the patron saint of the stew pot, as another legend says there was always a pot of stew on the go in their humble dwelling in Torrelaguna, outside Madrid. They welcomed anyone hungry and gave them a meal. No matter how many people arrived, every time María went to ladle out another portion of stew there was enough in the pot.

After Isidro's death María became a hermit, having visions of the Virgin Mary and performing miracles. She died many years later, in 1175, and was beatified by Pope Innocent XII in 1697. The remains of San Isidro and Santa María de la Cabeza are together in the Real Colegiata de San Isidoro in Madrid. Her statue can be seen on the Puente de Toledo and there are also charming polychrome figures of the saints in the Museo de San Isidro.

sanctuary of various European monarchs on the run. Under the Franco dictatorship exiled noteworthies including King Simeon of Bulgaria and Crown Prince Leka of Albania revelled in a life of peacocks and champagne corks, which never failed to enliven the pages of the fashion magazines.

Madrid was one of the least likely of townships to become a national capital, much less the nucleus of an empire. What put it on the map, so to speak, was location, location, location. A few kilometres to the south, in the district of Getafe, stands El Cerro de los Ángeles, a fourteenth-century hilltop monastery visible today from many of the city's fashionable rooftop bars. This is the geographic centre of the Iberian Peninsula. Bullet holes in the monastery walls attest to the Republican onslaught against the fascist-held site during the Spanish Civil War. It stands as a monument to scars that have yet to heal.

Madrid is a topographical as well as a political epicentre. The monumental Neoclassical building in the Puerta del Sol, with its celebrated bell tower that chimes in the New Year to thousands of revellers in the street, has gone through several incarnations in its 250-year history, from central post office to secret police headquarters during the Franco dictatorship, to its current use as the Madrid regional government headquarters. If you stand in front of its great iron gates, you will see the curious sight of crowds of passers-by stopping to take photos of the pavement. A brass plaque embedded in the street bears the inscription *Kilómetro Cero* (Kilometre Zero), set against a silhouette of the map of Spain. This is the starting point for the six major roads leading from Madrid to the Basque Country, Cataluña, Valencia, Andalucía, Extremadura and Galicia. The plaque, which was unveiled in 1950, also serves as a reference point for Madrid's street numbering, which had been introduced in the nineteenth century. Number 1 on the door of any house in the city marks the one closest to the Puerta del Sol; radiating outward, those on the left side of the street are odd numbered and those on the right even. Felipe II was aware of the advantages of Madrid's central location: the city stands equidistant from Spain's major ports and provided the monarch with a strategic position for exercising control over his domains.

Madrid's Kilometre Zero plaque.

In the space of some five hundred years, from the expulsion of the Moors by Alfonso VI in the eleventh century to the city's establishment as the capital by Felipe II, Magerit gradually transformed itself into Madrid, a prosperous town under the rule of a small clique of Castilian noblemen. If you should meet a native Madrileño bearing the surname Vargas, Arias, Luján or Mendoza, you can be reasonably certain that person's *gato* pedigree stretches back centuries into the city's history. These families offered hospitality to the frequent stopovers of the monarch and the attendant troupe of courtiers. This in turn gave rise to a craft industry of luxury items like fine woven goods, jewellery and works of art, all of which were much in demand among the court followers. The manufacture of these wares was by no means the exclusive domain of Castilian craftsmen. Archaeological digs have unearthed a network of workshops in areas which, in the Middle Ages, lay outside the city walls. These spaces were reserved for Jews and *Mudéjars*, the Muslims who stayed behind after the final expulsion in 1492. The ruling families of Madrid granted these two minorities right of abode, albeit only in their respective quarters, or ghettos to be more precise. The excavations also show that despite Madrid's deceptively flat landscape, the city was built on seven hills, like

Engraving
representing
Alfonso VI, seizing
Magerit from the
Moors.

Rome. The altitude difference between the Plaza de Castilla to the
north and one of the principal medieval Muslim quarters around
the Plaza de San Andrés to the south, measures 141 metres (465 ft).

The Jewish presence in Madrid dates to the city's conquest by
Christian forces in 1085, and probably even earlier. Alfonso vi had
taken Toledo from the Moors before marching on Magerit. The
Toledo ancestry of most of Madrid's medieval Jewish families attests
to a mass migration north in the late eleventh century, in the wake
of the advancing Christian armies. On their arrival, most of the Jews
settled around the Arab wall, traces of which are to be found at the
junction of the Calle Mayor and the Cuesta de la Vega. Here, alongside the oldest existing remnant of an Islamic wall in Spain, they set
up a small settlement, which centuries later became the site of the
Almudena Cathedral. As in most of Spain, the Jewish colony lived
near the seat of local government, where they carried out their

trades. The wall was adjacent to the Alcázar Palace, the fortress that had been built on this spot in the second half of the ninth century. Seven centuries later, after being razed to the ground in the infamous Christmas Eve fire that lasted four days, the fortress was replaced by the sprawl of the Royal Palace, the residence of the Bourbon monarchy.

The Habsburgs ruled for nearly two hundred years, from the uninspired reign of Felipe I 'The Handsome' in 1506, to the physically disabled and childless Carlos II, whose death in 1700 ignited the War of the Spanish Succession and heralded the arrival of the Bourbons at the court of Madrid. The first Felipe of the Habsburg dynasty never resided in the future capital. As king of Castile, before Spain was unified under a single crown in 1516, his was an itinerant court, moving as the fancy took him from Valladolid to Burgos and other cities across his realm. His son Carlos I, the Holy Roman Emperor Charles V, contributed little to Madrid's architectural heritage. His main achievement was to enlarge the Alcázar after it suffered extensive damage in the anti-government rising of 1520, known as the Revolt of the Comuneros.

It was under the later 'Felipes' that the monarchy took the initiative to bestow great monuments upon their capital, many of which have become enduring landmarks. One of Felipe II's concerns was to facilitate access to the city for travellers, grain and livestock from the town of Segovia, in the hills 100 kilometres (60 mi.) to the north. The king commissioned his favoured architect, Juan de Herrera, the creator of his El Escorial monastic retreat, to design a bridge for transporting goods and travellers across the Manzanares River. The Renaissance-style Puente de Segovia, Madrid's oldest surviving bridge, was completed in 1584, with nine brick and granite arches leading over the river to the hub of Madrid's historic Barrio de los Austrias.

Madrid grew and prospered after it became the country's capital. The city walls erected by Enrique II in the mid-fourteenth century, and enlarged by the Catholic Monarchs Fernando and Isabel a century later, proved too confining for a rapidly expanding population. Felipe II pushed back the perimeter of the old walls and added new gates. His aims were to deny access to victims of the plagues that periodically swept through other Castilian cities, set up tax collection points and provide Madrid's inhabitants with more living space. In all, the new walls enclosed an area of some 50 hectares (125 ac). By necessity, the expansion continued and was completed sixty years later by Felipe IV, known as 'the Great', who built a new wall encircling the urban area. By now, Madrid had expanded fourfold to 485 hectares (1,200 ac). The city's surrounding walls remained intact until the second half of the nineteenth century, when they were demolished, along with the gates that gave access to the city through what are today the Puerta del Sol, Puerta de Alcalá, Plaza de Antón Martín and several other spots now located in the city centre.

Equestrian statue of Felipe IV in the Plaza de Oriente.

Felipe III gave to Madrid a monument that symbolizes the grandeur of one of history's largest empires. The Plaza Mayor was the symbolic epicentre of the Spanish crown's imperial dominions, which extended from Latin America to Europe and the Far East. When completed in 1619, this enormous square covered nearly 18,500 square metres (200,000 sq. ft), enclosed by six-storey houses with a total of two hundred balconies, from which residents were entertained by spectacles from canonizations and public executions, to bullfights and royal coronations. The king's good work was commemorated by a bronze equestrian statue, which, alas, for many years served as a graveyard for sparrows. The death trap was revealed in 1931, with the proclamation of the Second Republic, when anti-monarchists dropped fireworks into the horse's mouth. The ensuing fire fractured the horse's side and hundreds of bird bones scattered across the paving stones. For centuries the birds had been flying unwarily into the mouth, since sealed, where they became trapped and died.

The Plaza Mayor drew praise from foreign visitors, notably French travellers of the eighteenth and nineteenth centuries. 'The surface area of the plaza is much vaster than any I have seen in Paris or elsewhere, and longer than it is wide,' wrote Henri de Saint-Simon in 1721. 'I was lost for words for seven or eight minutes.' For Alexandre Dumas, nearly a century later, 'The Plaza Mayor offers a unique spectacle, with its tiers, its balconies, its windows, its roofs full of spectators . . . More than 100,000 people could see and be seen.'

Apart from expanding the city walls to accommodate a growing population, Felipe IV can be credited with building Madrid's other great bridge, the Puente de Toledo. Unlike the Puente de Segovia, this project was dogged by misfortune from the placement of the first granite block in 1660. The structure was washed away several times by flash floods and the bridge we see today was not completed until 1732, in the reign of Felipe V, Madrid's first monarch of the Bourbon dynasty. In that year, the ornate Baroque statues of Madrid's patron saint San Isidro and his canonized wife Santa María de la Cabeza were placed halfway across the span. The Puente de

Segovia and, to the south, that of Toledo gave access to the city along the streets of the same names, which converge at a point near Plaza de la Puerta Cerrada, in La Latina district. Despite his bad luck with the Puente de Toledo, Felipe IV will be remembered as a patron of the arts, in particular the court painter Diego Velázquez, and a supporter of Madrid's celebrated playwrights of the day. Not to be outdone by his father, Felipe III, in 1616 he commissioned the Italian sculptor Pietro Tacca to execute an even grander equestrian statue of his royal personage, which stands majestically in the gardens of the Plaza de Oriente, facing the Royal Palace. The king wanted the horse to be rearing on its hind legs, a sculptural feat that had never been achieved before. Tacca sought advice from Galileo Galilei on how to ensure the huge structure's stability. The solution was to make the rear part of the horse solid and the front hollow, with its bronze tail acting as an additional counterweight. Madrid historian Corpus Barga considers this an outstanding example of equestrian statues. 'The horse and rider not only represent the best equestrian statue in Madrid, but one of the finest worldwide,' he says. 'Some even consider it superior to the Coleone in Venice. It reflects the genius of Velázquez, and his two paintings that served as models for Pietro Tacca.'

2 The Golden Age of Empire and Literature

Luis de Góngora and Francisco de Quevedo have three things in common. They are acknowledged as the greatest Baroque poets of Spain's Siglo de Oro, the Golden Age of literature that stretches roughly from the late sixteenth to the end of the seventeenth centuries. Góngora and Quevedo lived as neighbours in the centre of the Barrio de las Letras, Madrid's historic literary quarter. They also shared a deep-rooted loathing of one another.

The two poets enjoyed great fame and royal patronage in Spain's Baroque age. They were favoured by Felipe III and followed the king to Valladolid when he relocated his capital from Madrid to the northern city from 1601 to 1606. The move had been inspired by the omnipotent royal counsellor, the Duke of Lerma, for reasons that have never been fully clarified. The duke owned several stately residences in Valladolid, so property speculation cannot be ruled out as a motivating force, as he would have been aware of the upward pressure the court presence would put on the value of homes in the city.

Like so many of Spain's literati, past and present, Góngora was an immigrant to Madrid. He came from the sumptuous and cultured city of Córdoba, a centre of European arts and natural science since the middle ages. Córdoba's sensuous poetic tradition shines through in his work, known as *culteranismo*, or 'cultured verse'. Quevedo, the club-footed, myopic bard whose name became synonymous with the pince-nez he wore, was a native Madrileño. His swashbuckling life as a swordsman and frequent visitor to Madrid brothels and taverns was reflected in his manner of verse, called *conceptismo* (conceptualism), characterized by an acerbic wit and directness. To the delight

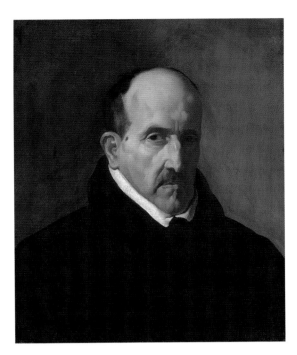

Luis de Góngora, painted by Velázquez, 1622.

of Madrid's reading public, these two early seventeenth-century poets became engaged in a duel of sonnets. Góngora focused on disparaging Quevedo's poetic talents, while his rival fired off fourteen-line broadsides aimed not only at Góngora's poetry, but his person as well. The battle came to a head when Quevedo published a sonnet heaping scorn on Góngora for his alleged Jewish ancestry, a dangerous accusation in seventeenth-century Spain. In *A una nariz* (To a Nose), Quevedo writes:

> *Érase un espolón de una galera,*
> *érase una pirámide de Egipto,*
> *las doce tribus de narices era.*

> It [Góngora's nose] was a galleon's spur,
> It was a pyramid of Egypt,
> It was the Twelve Tribes of noses.

Not satisfied with these literary fusillades, when Quevedo found out that his enemy had lost a fortune at cards and was living in humble rented accommodation in Madrid's Barrio de las Letras, he audaciously purchased the house and had him evicted. The ochre stone house at number seven, Calle del Niño, directly opposite the Trinitarias Convent, has been ignominiously renamed calle de Quevedo. There is a plaque on the building's facade, located above a lively bar and restaurant, to commemorate the poet's life in the neighbourhood. There is no mention of the fact that this was originally Góngora's home.

To the dismay and bewilderment of many of its long-time residents, the Barrio de las Letras, like many of Madrid's historic quarters, has become a showpiece of gentrification and trendiness. The boutique and smart café-sprinkled streets like Calle del León and Calle de las Huertas present a vivid contrast of bearded and tattooed newcomers to elderly people in woolly tartan slippers for whom the confines of the neighbourhood delineate their universe.

Francisco de Quevedo, painted by Rafael Ximeno, 1791.

Few cities can boast a literary quarter sparkling with such a vast array of creativity as was the case with Madrid's Barrio de las Letras in the seventeenth century. Quevedo and Góngora lived in this small neighbourhood, which extends from the Puerta del Sol eastward to the Paseo del Prado, bounded north and south respectively by Carrera de San Jerónimo and Calle de Atocha. The barrio can be traversed on foot in any direction in no more than fifteen minutes. But these two poets were not the only luminaries to be seen drinking in the taverns, holding court on street corners or simply running their daily errands in the narrow cobbled lanes around the Trinitarias Convent.

The Barrio de las Letras was in fact a very small space to contain the egos of Spain's immortal giants of Golden Age literature. This triangular district, bordered to the north by the Carrera de San Jerónimo and to the south by the Calle de Alcalá, is known to this day by its original name. Printers had their workshops here and bookshops were later to proliferate, but the area's literary character was consolidated above all by its theatres, which lent the area a reputation for being Bohemian, loose-living and pleasure-seeking.

At the turn of the seventeenth century, Miguel de Cervantes, whose *Don Quijote* remains the world's most widely read novel, and Félix Lope de Vega, one of history's most prolific dramatists, maintained at the best of times a sneering relationship with one another. Lope is reputed to have written up to 1,500 plays, though none ever achieved the degree of worldwide acclaim of his rival's novel of the tragicomic knight errant. The print shop that gave birth to this two-part tale of decadent chivalry, Antigua Imprenta Juan de la Cuesta, has been preserved for visits behind a narrow oak door, sandwiched between construction materials workshops in Calle de San Eugenio. Another irony of nomenclature is the Calle de Cervantes, which happens to be the street on which Lope lived. His home at number 11, now a museum open to the public, is a brick-fronted affair where the playwright spent his days, writing furiously in the upstairs study, right up until his death in 1635. Cervantes's tribute to his neighbour was the ambiguous accolade 'Monster of Nature'. This could be taken as an acknowledgement of his prodigious literary output, or equally as a jibe at Lope's notorious

womanizing. Despite the many well-publicized scandals of his life, Lope arose as a giant in the eye of Madrid's theatre-goers. His portrait hung in hundreds of salons, while adoring fans would rush up to kiss his hand in the street. Yet not a trace is left of Spain's most celebrated dramatist, for Lope's remains were lost when the graveyard of his local church was demolished to make way for a florist's shop. Not so Cervantes, whose skeleton was identified by a team of archaeologists in 2015 in the crypt of the Trinitarias Convent, which stands, as one might guess, in Calle Lope de Vega.

In the years before the Golden Age, Felipe II gave scant thought to smartening up his imperial capital. When not administering his empire, the king's mind was fixed on the construction of his El Escorial mountain monastic retreat. This was a Herculean task involving exceptional names of the day, foremost of whom was the architect Juan Bautista de Toledo (also known as Giovanni Battista de Alfonsis), a disciple of Michelangelo, as well as Juan de Herrera and Giovanni Battista Castello, an acclaimed architect residing in the Spanish possession of Naples. The sober grey stone favoured by Herrera was dragged from a granite quarry across hilly ground by teams of up to fifty oxen. Marble for the interior walls was hauled from surrounding regions, along with sumptuous tapestries from Granada and Seville. This was a project of international dimensions, with tropical timber and ebony used to fashion the beams and panelling, being brought by galleon from the South American colonies. Whatever changes came about to Madrid under this most austere of the Habsburg monarchs were almost exclusively to satisfy Felipe's personal interests. The king was a fanatic of the hunt, and to provide himself with a suitable hunting ground he established the Casa de Campo, the vast park west of the city that can now be reached by cable car. Felipe also extended to the outskirts of the city the hunting grounds of the fifteenth-century Royal Pardo Palace on Madrid's northern outskirts, the official residence of General Francisco Franco until his death in 1975.

Felipe II's influence in Madrid fell well short of expectations. The city's population soared fivefold during his nearly forty years on the throne. However, apart from perfunctory attempts at urban

The Cervantes monument in the Plaza de España, with figures of Don Quijote and Sancho Panza.

renewal – such as extending the Calle de Segovia from its start at the new bridge over the Manzanares River, or the demolition of sections of the city wall to give access to the Calle Mayor which in 1570 had served with much solemnity as the royal entrance for the king's fourth wife, his niece Anna of Austria – almost nothing was done to address the need to build homes for the city's increasingly numerous inhabitants. Lacking enough housing, much of late seventeenth-century Madrid, the capital of an empire that spanned five continents, resembled a shanty town, lacking sanitation, street lighting or any semblance of a civic consciousness. Madrid was, by all accounts, the dirtiest capital in Europe. Envisaging this state of abandonment requires a major stretch of the imagination, in a city whose streets are now hosed down every morning and which boasts the greatest number of trees of any European capital: some 30 per cent of Madrid is green area, home to nearly 300,000 trees without counting parkland. This was not the case until the mid-nineteenth century, a time when trees were conspicuous by their absence from the city, other than in the Retiro Park or Paseo del Prado.

Urban improvements under Felipe II were carried out almost exclusively on royal quarters. San Jerónimo el Real rises dramatically on a hillock behind the Prado Museum, next to where the Buen Retiro Royal Palace was situated before it was destroyed in the early nineteenth-century French occupation of Madrid. The original church had been built in 1505 by the Catholic monarchs Fernando and Isabel and it soon became the established place of worship of the nobility, who went there to swear allegiance to the crown princes of Castile. Felipe II had the retreat enlarged to become the Buen Retiro Palace, where he established his quarters next to the presbytery so that he could hear Mass from his bedroom. The king retreated to Los Jerónimos for Easter services and other solemn occasions. The edifice was left in a state of semi-abandonment until the nineteenth century, when major restoration works were twice undertaken, on both occasions in neo-Gothic style, leaving intact only a few external features of the church's original structure.

Felipe II was obsessed with living up to the legacy of his formidable father Carlos I, who had ruled over the Holy Roman as well as Spanish empires. Carlos's extension of the Alcázar was the first and most important step taken to renovate the interior as well as the building's exterior facade. Felipe was determined to do one better than his father, and he spent nearly four decades, until his death in 1598, having the austere fortress converted to a royal palace worthy of the title. Under the supervision of Gaspar de la Vega, the court architect who had implemented Emperor Carlos's reforms, Felipe brought in masons, glaziers, carpenters, painters, sculptors and other artisans from across Europe. Juan Bautista de Toledo, for instance, the chief design architect of El Escorial, executed the Torre Dorada (Golden Tower), which was the Alcázar's *pièce de résistance* until its destruction in the fire of 1734.

Felipe III succeeded his father in 1598 at the age of twenty. Three years after ascending the throne, he took the remarkable decision to move his court from Madrid to Valladolid. The ancient Castilian city 200 kilometres (125 mi.) northwest of Madrid had long been a favourite residence of Spain's rulers, from the Catholic Monarchs of the fifteenth century to Carlos I. Apart from the mighty and influential Duke of Lerma's real-estate interests, the move might have been motivated by the rundown state of Madrid, as well as Valladolid's less extreme climate and abundant supply of water from the nearby Duero River. Thus, on a bitterly cold January morning in 1601, the day after the official proclamation was issued, the royal court was once again on the march, forty years after the dusty trek from Toledo to Madrid. Felipe III achieved little of lasting note in the five years he reigned in Valladolid. He dispatched the imperial army to lay siege to Ostend, he forged a military alliance with Persia against the Ottoman Empire, a rebellion was crushed in the Philippines and, arguably most significant of all, in August 1604 he signed the Treaty of London at Somerset House, which concluded nearly twenty years of warfare with England. Seven months after sealing the peace settlement, the king gathered his host for the journey back to his native city of Madrid.

Just as his father's decision to make Madrid his capital has never been conclusively explained, Felipe III's reasons for taking the court back to Madrid are shrouded in mystery. In the

The Church of Los Jerónimos, behind the Prado museum.

time-honoured tradition of Habsburg inbreeding, a year after his coronation Felipe III married his cousin, the Austrian archduchess Margaret. As had been the case with his father's wife, Elisabeth de Valois, the Holy Roman Emperor's granddaughter was an influential figure at Felipe III's court. She was an astute manipulator who nursed a strong dislike of the Duke of Lerma. It is not inconceivable that Margaret would have schemed to engineer the move away from Valladolid with the express aim of undermining the duke's political position. The plague epidemic that swept across northern Castile from 1602 may well have been another compelling motivation for quitting the city.

Felipe showed himself to be an uninspired monarch, a man of an apathetic disposition who took little interest in his responsibilities. His father, Felipe II, did not fail to note these shortcomings, and on more than one occasion he confided his concerns to those close to him at court. Following Felipe II's death, the country's affairs were left effectively in the hands of the Duke of Lerma, a despot detested by numerous scions of Madrid's nobility and influential figures at court, who, led by the duke's own son, finally succeeded in engineering his downfall in 1618. Only the duke's status as cardinal

THE ATENEO

The showpiece of the Barrio de las Letras is the Ateneo, or to give it its full name in English, the Artistic, Scientific and Literary Athenaeum. The Ateneo was founded in 1820 as a liberal sanctuary for the promotion of arts and letters, and was summarily shut down by Fernando VII, the reactionary monarch who ruled twice, for a year in 1808 and again from 1814 to 1833. Two years after the tyrant's death, the Ateneo re-opened and later moved to its present headquarters at Calle del Prado, where it stands in the very core of the barrio. The gated, modernist entrance leads up an imposing flight of marble steps into a world that echoes with intellectual glories, past and present. Members can ascend yet another staircase to the magnificent library, where a single word uttered above a whisper will ignite a clicking of tongues, exasperated sighs and fiery glares from researchers hunched in their cubicles. Those who do not hold the coveted membership card can soak up the Ateneo's nineteenth-century splendour in the downstairs café and bistro.

Many leading writers, including the master of nineteenth-century realism Benito Pérez Galdós and the radical dramatist Ramón María del Valle-Inclán, as well as prime ministers and all Spanish Nobel Prize winners, were to be found late into the night in the Ateneo's smoke-filled salons, which hummed with a lively exchange of views on literature and politics. The Ateneo's lecture theatre has over the years hosted international greats of the arts and sciences, from Sarah Bernhardt to Albert Einstein. It remains one of Madrid's foremost focal points of cultural activities, featuring recitals, *tertulias* (literary and political debates), art shows and poetry readings.

LA BIBLIOTECA.—(DIBUJO DEL NATURAL, POR M. ALCÁZAR.)

Bernardo Rico, *The Library of the Ateneo*, 1884, engraving.

Plaza Mayor, showing Felipe III's visit, 14 May 1619.

gave him immunity from prosecution. Margaret did not live to see her vengeful dreams fulfilled, for she had died in childbirth seven years previously, leaving Felipe III a widower for the rest of his life. The years of Felipe's reign following his wife's death were characterized by a tenuous peace in Spain's European possessions and the countries of the West. This came to a violent end in 1618 with the outbreak of the Thirty Years' War, in which Felipe gave his unconditional support to the Holy Roman Emperor. The religious conflict saw 8 million fatalities and, for Spain, the loss of Portugal and the Low Countries. Felipe III further enfeebled his kingdom with the expulsion of the Moriscos, those Moors who had converted to Christianity. This was a blunder almost on a scale with the Catholic monarchs' edict of expulsion of the Jews a century earlier. Both acts of religious fanaticism caused Spain serious economic and demographic difficulties, by depopulating areas of the country, although Felipe had reason to suspect the Moriscos were conspiring with French Huguenots against the Habsburg dynasty.

The monarch's most outstanding bequest to Madrid was conceived and carried out after his return from Valladolid. It was resolved by royal decree that Spain's now permanent capital must be endowed with a central square, surpassing in grandeur that of Valladolid. Thus in 1617 work commenced on an enlarged Plaza Mayor, the symbolic centre of the Spanish Empire, to replace the one erected during his father's reign. The finished square occupies 12,075 square metres (130,000 sq. ft) and as such it is over 2,000 square metres (24,000 sq. ft) larger than its northern rival, which at the time of its completion had been the largest public square in Spain. Originally an arena for bullfighting, jousting and public executions, four centuries later the Plaza Mayor remains the most celebrated landmark of Madrid's historic old town.

Felipe III died at the relatively young age of 43, allegedly after scorching himself on a coal brazier in his Alcázar Palace. In 1621 his teenage son Felipe IV ascended the throne in an overcrowded city that had deteriorated to a shambolic state of filth and neglect. The impoverished and in many cases disease-stricken provinces were being depopulated at an alarming rate during Felipe IV's reign, as people flocked to Madrid, swelling the population of the capital to 140,000. Though outwardly still the world's supreme imperial power, the benefits of empire had grown conspicuous by their absence. Gold and silver looted from the colonies and carted to Madrid by mule train from Seville and Cádiz vanished down a sinkhole of mismanagement and was squandered on foreign wars. The king was a man obsessed with death, who fathered some thirty illegitimate children and spent much of his time lying in his funeral niche in El Escorial monastery. Given his tormented state of mind, Felipe IV fell easy prey to his cunning favourite, Gaspar de Guzmán, Count-Duke of Olivares, who swiftly became the true power behind the throne.

Olivares persuaded the king to raise an adobe wall, known as a *cerca*, around Madrid's populated area. This was done to protect the city from plague-carriers, and also as a barrier to contraband goods and the influx of criminals and other undesirables. The north and south extents of the wall corresponded roughly to today's roadways of Los Bulevares and Las Rondas. The western perimeter ran alongside the Manzanares River and to the east, the Retiro Park.

In all, the *cerca de Felipe IV*, as it was known, enclosed an area of some 800 hectares (2,000 ac), almost half of which was Crown property.

Leaving aside character failings, of which there were many, the one redeeming virtue common to the 'Felipes' was their support of the arts. Felipe II was a lifelong collector of works by Titian and his affection for the bizarre manifested itself in a love of the works of Hieronymus Bosch, especially *The Garden of Earthly Delights* triptych (1503–15) that hung in his Escorial bedroom. Felipe III was an admirer of Rubens, whose work is well-represented in the Prado Museum today. Felipe IV's enthusiasm for the great painters went a step beyond patronage. The monarch's close personal association with Diego Velázquez was virtually unique in the history of art. For his part, Velázquez played his hand with caution. In his masterwork *Las Meninas* (1656) the artist felt comfortable enough to place himself on the same canvas as the king. Velázquez also produced ten portraits of Felipe IV, half a dozen of the monarch's son Baltasar Carlos and, to be on the safe side, an equal number of the king's favourite, the Count-Duke Olivares. The artist took pains to ensure his equestrian portraits were perfect in every detail. Viewers can spot the pentimenti (traces of earlier painting beneath the final image) on some of his canvases. Velázquez would make subtle corrections in the placement of a horse, for instance, or even the curve of a horse's tail, and over time the painted-over marks would become visible on the painting's surface. The changes are especially noticeable in the portraits of Felipe IV.

More than two centuries of Habsburg rule in Spain came crashing down in 1700, when Felipe IV's only surviving son, Carlos II (nicknamed 'the Bewitched'), a man tormented by physical and mental afflictions, succumbed to an agonizing death. On his deathbed Carlos II named as his heir Philippe, Duke of Anjou. Philippe, an exalted member of the French royal family, would rule as Felipe V. He spoke not a word of Spanish. In short order Europe was plunged into a full-blown crisis over rival claims to the Spanish throne. The Bourbons had been sharpening their knives ever since it became apparent that Carlos II, who could hardly stand erect or utter an intelligible word, was incapable of producing an heir. It was clear that claims to the Spanish crown would soon become the *casus belli* for a general European conflagration. On one side there was the Grand Alliance, comprising Britain, the United Provinces of the Netherlands and Austria's Holy Roman Empire. The northern Dutch provinces had seceded from the Habsburg Netherlands, which was ruled by Madrid, in 1648. The Bourbon camp brought together France, those Spanish loyal to Louis xiv's grandson Philip v, and their Bavarian allies. Spain still held the southern, Catholic provinces of the Netherlands, including the powerful county of Flanders. After thirteen years of all-out European conflagration in 1714 the Treaty of Baden concluded hostilities between Bourbon France and the pro-Habsburg Grand Alliance. The Spanish Habsburgs were no more. The result of this war was the official enthronement of Felipe v and the start of more than three centuries of intermittent Bourbon rule, which, except for the interlude of two Republics and the Franco regime, continues to the present day.

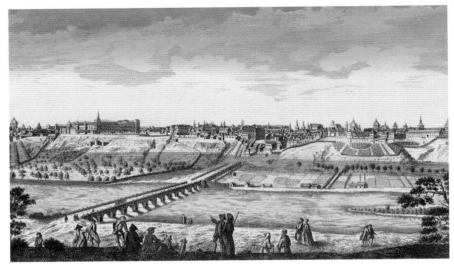

General view of Madrid, after an engraving published in 1762.

3 City of Enlightenment

The very mention of the name 'Bourbon' triggers a knee-jerk reaction in numerous Madrileños. The people of Madrid tend to associate this dynasty with moral decadence or, in the most recalcitrant of collective memories, with a French army of occupation that held the capital under its thumb from 1808 to 1812 in the Napoleonic Wars. The first allegation is largely groundless, the second is a fact of history. What is often overlooked is that the arrival of the Bourbons brought a breath of fresh air to the development of the arts and architecture. It was this change of royal dynasty that catapulted Madrid to its status as a truly world-class city. 'In 1700, Madrid was still an insalubrious and disorganised city, lacking urban amenities such as paved roads or a sewage system,' according to historians Fernando Revilla and Rosalía Ramos. 'The Bourbon court immediately recognised that this was an inappropriate state of affairs for the capital.'

Felipe V ruled Spain for nearly half a century, from 1700 to 1746. He is the longest-reigning monarch in modern Spanish history. His years on the throne overlapped with the most spirited days of the European Enlightenment, whose values of knowledge, reason and individualism were introduced to the court of Madrid. This was in sharp contrast with the religious intolerance and intellectual stupor that had characterized much of Spain's Habsburg years. The king brought new ideas, architects and painters from France and Italy, and the new royal family busied themselves giving Madrid a contemporary Neoclassical carapace.

In keeping with the tradition of his native France, Felipe V set about centralizing Spain's system of government. This greatly

LAVAPIÉS

Lavapiés is one of Madrid's most ethnically diverse neighbourhoods, and one of its oldest. The district lies in the city's southeast sector, a maze of steep, winding streets, whose inhabitants lived in *corralas*, residential blocks arranged around an interior courtyard. The most famous one still standing is located on the corner of Calle del Tribulete and Calle de Mesón de Paredes. After the expulsion of the Jews in 1492, Lavapiés's social profile moved from being a Jewish ghetto to the home of Madrid's *conversos* (Jews who converted to Catholicism, known as new Christians). The name 'Lavapiés' translates as 'feet wash', believed to be a reference to a fountain in which Christians visiting the ghetto would wash their feet upon leaving. It is far more likely that the Jews made use of the fountain when returning after a business excursion to the city.

Lavapiés has always been on the fringes of Madrid, socially as well as geographically. The neighbourhood developed outside the walled town after Madrid became the capital in 1561. It attracted the poorest segments of society, as more affluent Madrileños were loath to live at a lower physical elevation than the Royal Palace and districts of the higher social classes. In the late nineteenth and early twentieth centuries it was Lavapiés's working-class character that inspired some of Madrid's most famous *zarzuelas*, or light operettas, like *El barberillo de Lavapiés* (The Little Barber of Lavapiés) and *El conde de Lavapiés* (The Count of Lavapiés). In spite of the proliferation in the 1980s and '90s of trendy bars and cafés, Lavapiés has lost none of its diversity. Since then the massive influx of Chinese, Indians, Senegalese and Moroccans – in all, more than eighty different nationalities – have made Lavapiés Madrid's most international barrio.

Vibrant, multicultural Lavapiés.

enhanced the power and influence of Madrid over other cities – including in several cases, it must be said, more eminent ones, such as Valladolid and Toledo. Felipe's model was the political consolidation that had been imposed by his grandfather Louis XIV of France. To this end he abolished the charters of all independently administered kingdoms, with the exception of Navarre and the Basque region, the two areas that had supported Felipe's cause in the war for the Spanish throne.

The early eighteenth century ushered in the dawn of Madrid's age of architectural glory. The motivating force behind this building boom was Francisco Antonio de Salcedo y Aguirre, Marquis of Vadillo. Salcedo was a scion of the Castilian nobility and had championed Felipe's claim to the throne during the War of the Spanish Succession. The king repaid his loyalty by appointing Salcedo as Madrid's *Corregidor*, a post equivalent to chief magistrate, which in 1803 became the office of mayor. Salcedo's first important commission was the construction of a barracks to accommodate Felipe V's six-hundred-strong Royal Guard, with stables for four hundred horses. The Cuartel del Conde Duque, which occupies a 230-metre-long (750-ft) swathe of the street of the same name, is a colossal yet well-proportioned complex. It was begun in 1717 and took nearly twenty years to complete. Salcedo did not live to see his epic project in its finished state. The stern-faced city chief administrator, with his steely eyes and great snowy wig, is immortalized in a portrait by the court painter Miguel Jacinto Meléndez, which hangs in the Madrid Municipal Museum in Calle de Fuencarral. Salcedo died in 1729 at the unusually ripe old age of 82. Were he alive today, he could take pride in his achievement: Conde Duque is now a Spanish Heritage Site and one of Madrid's foremost cultural centres. The buildings surrounding its great cobbled courtyard hold the Madrid municipal archives, a cinema and theatre, a conference centre, Madrid's Contemporary Arts Museum and an engaging replica of the cluttered and richly ornamented office of the twentieth-century writer and avant-garde agitator Ramón Gómez de la Serna.

Salcedo's principal attainment was to have brought on board Pedro de Ribera to design Conde Duque, the architect's tour de force. Over the subsequent years, Ribera would build numerous bridges, fountains, churches, palaces and public buildings throughout Madrid. He was awarded the title of *Arquitecto de la Villa*, or chief architect of the city, in recognition of his work as the leading Baroque draughtsman of his day. Ribera's impact on Madrid was unique among Spanish architects. The son of a working-class family in the deeply *castizo* (traditional) district of Lavapiés, Ribera worked as apprentice to José Benito de Churriguera and Teodoro Ardemans, the two most prestigious architects of his day. It was not until he was 36 that Ribera was commissioned to design the Conde Duque barracks. In his comparatively short, 25-year career, until his death in 1742, Ribera designed or carried out improvements on at least 22 major buildings and monuments in and around Madrid. His work brought a revolutionary makeover to a city suffering from decades of neglect and decrepitude.

It is not unusual for visitors to Madrid to stand in astonishment in front of the History of Madrid Museum, originally the Royal Hospice, in Calle de Fuencarral. Before them stands Ribera's towering, elaborate Baroque entrance, contrasting sharply with the sobriety of the building's Neoclassical facade. One gets the impression that the architect took out everything in his pockets to attach to this fantasy in stone. The elaborate portal is described as creating illusions, with its imitations of the folds and tassels of curtains in stone. From street level to roof, the great entranceway's oak doors are flanked by a profusion of statuettes, coats of arms, lobulated apertures and festoons, all of which are reminiscent of a cathedral altarpiece. Quite probably the intention was to simulate an altar retablo, or devotional painting, as well as to surprise with art. In this way, it reminds the passer-by of the religious foundation and charitable nature of the institution it was built to house.

Ribera's most prominent religious work is to be found in three Madrid churches: the Hermitage of the Vírgen del Puerto, the Temple of the Order of Theatines (a religious order founded in the sixteenth century by Pope Paul IV) and the Temple of the Convent of the Discalced Carmelites, now the Church of San José. The hermitage, located in the Paseo de la Vírgen del Puerto, close to the Royal

Palace, is a reconstruction of the original Ribera design and ranks as one of Spain's earliest examples of Baroque religious architecture. In its design, the structure bears a resemblance to a country park pavilion, with its trio of almost carnivalesque roof turrets. For centuries it was a destination for pilgrims, who trekked to Madrid to worship at the shrine located by the church altar. Salcedo was so taken by Ribera's feat that he chose the church as his final resting place.

The Temple of the Order of Theatines, now the Church of San Cayetano, stands in Calle de Embajadores in Madrid's southern district, a short walk from the Rastro flea market. Ribera is believed to have worked on the church's design in collaboration with the architects José Benito de Churriguera and Fernando Moradillo, but the basic inspiration came from Ribera himself. An extraordinary aspect of the building is the sensation it gives of being off-centre, with the great dome placed above the transept and close to the entranceway. Almost all the works of art in the church, along with the main altarpiece, were lost in a fire that destroyed the building during the Spanish Civil War of 1936–9. The new altar is a replacement executed in Baroque style, displaying copies of famous paintings that hang in the Prado Museum. One of the chapels contains the tomb of Ribera, who lived in a house facing the church at which he was a lifelong worshipper.

The Church of San José is found in Calle de Alcalá, in the very centre of Madrid, facing the Bank of Spain and a two-minute walk from the start of the Gran Vía. Its original, rather unwieldy name was the Temple of the Convent of the Discalced Carmelites of San Hermenegildo. It was founded by Felipe III in 1605 to commemorate the birth of his son, the future Felipe IV. In 1740 the nuns decided to renovate their convent. They had little choice in the matter, for the enormous building was crumbling to pieces. By the mid-eighteenth century, little was left of the original structure. The project was given to Ribera, whose style at this late stage in his career had begun to shift away from the Baroque towards a

Pedro de Ribera's ornate entrance to the Royal Hospice, now the History of Madrid Museum.

curvaceous Rococo. The convent's dome is not the simple design of the traditional Madrid church, but is instead adorned with intricate depictions of scattered leaves, decorated sashes and cherubim.

This was Ribera's last great undertaking, which was completed by his collaborator José de Arredondo after the master architect's death in 1742. The church's facade was raised in 1912 to keep it level with the first building in the Gran Vía, the avenue that opened up traffic through Madrid's commercial district in the early twentieth century.

Ribera's creative hand can be observed in other architectural gems of Madrid's 'Bourbon' century. He designed and built the Palacio de Miraflores in the Carrera de San Jerónimo, a short distance up the hill from the Spanish Parliament. The stately mansion was completed in 1732 after only two years of construction, and served as the residence of the count of Villapaterna, who was later granted the title of Marquis of Miraflores. The extensive three-storey rectangular house sits on a granite skirting, with a profusely decorated portal reaching up to the main balcony, very much in the Ribera style. The building remained in the Miraflores family for more than two hundred years, when it was sold and converted into an office block.

Many great institutions of learning and the arts were created under the patronage of Felipe v. The Bourbon monarch and the two kings who immediately followed him, Fernando vi and Carlos iii, bequeathed to Madrid the intellectual gifts of the European Enlightenment. In 1712, with the War of the Spanish Succession raging across Europe, the king issued a decree establishing the Biblioteca Nacional de España, the National Library of Spain. This immense Neoclassical building sits majestically in the Paseo de Recoletos, the tree-lined boulevard that bisects Madrid on a north–south axis. The steps leading up to the three towering iron gates impose a sense of awe on the visitor. Statues of Madrid's patron saint, San Isidro, and King Alfonso el Sabio (the Wise) stand guard, with Lope de Vega and Cervantes rising behind. The king founded the library because he wanted to encourage learning among his subjects. In this same vein, he established two further centres of erudition and scholarship, the Royal Academy of the Spanish Language in 1713 and the Royal Academy of History in 1738, both close to the Prado Museum. But there was another, more political motive behind Felipe's establishing a national library: the plan was to bring together the libraries of nobles who had fled the country after fighting on the side of the Habsburg pretender to the throne. The Biblioteca Nacional became Spain's first copyright library when Felipe v issued a Royal Letters Patent requiring printers to send to Madrid a copy of all new books printed in Spain. In more recent times, during the Spanish Civil War, some 500,000 volumes held in churches, palaces and private residences, along with numerous works of art, were removed to the library to save them from destruction. The National Library today ranks eleventh in the world for its number of holdings, with a collection of more than 33 million items.

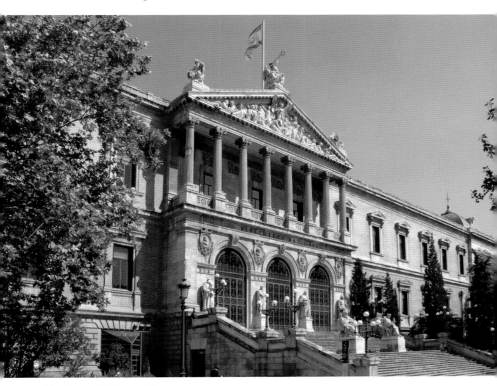

The National Library of Spain.

In 1719 Spain and its former possession of Flanders, which had declared its independence in 1581, broke off commercial relations in a trade dispute. This meant that the much-coveted Flemish tapestries were no longer exported to Spain. Two years later Felipe v founded the Real Fábrica de Tapices (Royal Tapestry Factory) in today's Plaza de Santa Bárbara. In 1889 the premises relocated to Calle de Fuenterrabía, near the Atocha Railway Station. The factory was set up under the direction of the Flemish Vandergoten family of master tapestry artisans, primarily to provide decorative works for the king's palace and other royal residences outside the capital. Spanish artists, including Goya, were commissioned to contribute designs to be woven into tapestries. These can still be admired by the public in the factory's museum. To this day, the factory continues to produce handmade tapestries and serves as a training centre for new weavers.

The crowning jewel of Madrid's architectural renaissance was the Palacio Real, the august Neoclassical Royal Palace whose rear gardens overlook the Manzanares River and, to the front, the Plaza de Oriente and Teatro Real. The square itself was planned to provide a dramatic view of the immense palace. Until the early nineteenth century, the east facade was obscured by a cluster of derelict houses, one of which had been the property of Diego Velázquez. With the Alcázar reduced to a pile of ashes in the fire of 1734, Felipe v commissioned the famed Sicilian architect Filippo Juvarra to come up with a design for a new royal residence. Within months Juvarra had arrived in Madrid. What he envisaged was a magnificent structure, in his estimation befitting the ruler of the Spanish Empire, which at that time included Sicily. The architect's sudden death less than a year after setting up his Madrid studio left the plans for the palace in the hands of his disciple and fellow Italian Juan Bautista Sachetti, who is considered the true genius behind the project. Juvarra had originally selected a site in the city's northern district. This was opposed by the king, who wanted it to rise, phoenix-like, on the ruins of the Alcázar. The monarch's will prevailed, though the final design called for a palace on a more modest scale than Juvarra had intended.

For the next 23 years, a 13-hectare (33-ac) area extending from the river to roughly the end of today's Calle del Arenal was turned into a vast building site. Felipe and his family moved into more modest quarters in the Palacio del Buen Retiro, the secondary royal residence built on what was the city's eastern limit. A constant stream of oxen wagons, day after day, hauled tonnes of granite from the Guadarrama hills to erect the imposing four-storey east facade, while cartloads of marble were brought from the quarries of the outlying village of Colmenar. On completion, the 3,418-room palace dazzled Madrileños with its Corinthian columns, soaring pilasters and, for those fortunate enough to catch a glimpse of the building's interior, the staircase of honour, designed by yet another Italian architect, Francesco Sabatini. The Palacio Real radically transformed Madrid's western contour, and over the course of time opened up new space for residential buildings by clearing adjacent land for its construction. Felipe v was not fated to take up residence in his new royal residence. When the king died in 1746 and his son Fernando vi ascended the throne, the palace remained an uninhabitable work in progress.

In stark contrast to his father's 46 years on the throne, Fernando vi ruled for only thirteen years, the shortest reign of any Bourbon monarch. Yet Madrid benefited greatly from the king, also known as 'the Learned', in this brief period. In 1752, the king created the Royal Academy of Bellas Artes (Fine Arts) of San Fernando, the Baroque building in the Calle de Alcalá by the Puerta del Sol. It now serves as a gallery and museum, housing a collection of sixteenth- to nineteenth-century paintings by Rubens, Zurbarán, Velázquez and other masters, including thirteen by Francisco de Goya, who was an academy member. In that same year, Fernando also founded the Giro Real, the precursor of Spain's future central bank. The rationale for taking this step was to ensure that public and private funds held outside Spain in foreign exchange were placed in the hands of the Royal Treasury, thereby enriching the state coffers. It is considered the predecessor to the Bank of San Carlos, introduced during the reign of Carlos iii.

Fernando was also a great believer in cultural advancement. The noted Italian composer Giuseppe Domenico Scarlatti (1685–1757),

The Royal Palace and paved forecourt.

who spent much of his life in the service of the Spanish royal family, wrote many of his 555 keyboard sonatas at the court of Madrid. Scarlatti also served as music teacher to the king's wife, the Portuguese princess Barbara de Braganza.

The court of Fernando VI was not without its political intrigues. One of the most prominent figures during his reign was Zenón de Somodevilla, Marquess of Ensenada, Secretary of the Treasury, Navy and Indies. Ensenada was instrumental in persuading the king of the need to modernize Spain. First and foremost was the task of maintaining a position of strength abroad, to ensure that France and Great Britain acknowledged Spain as a formidable power. It was largely through Ensenada's efforts and deployment of a great fleet to patrol the seas that Spain was able to enjoy years of tranquillity and economic recovery. This was one of the few times in Spanish history when a monarch ruled over a country at peace. The economy was the great beneficiary of these years, when Spain was not obliged to divert large sums from the treasury to finance military adventures in Europe. The cutbacks in military expenditure in turn stimulated an economic recovery which, in the case of Madrid, yielded the municipal treasury's first recorded budget surplus. Ensenada was a supporter of Louis xv of France, while his rival at court, José de Carvajal y Lancáster, First Secretary of State, advocated Spain's alliance with Great Britain. The long-running feud between the two officials came to an abrupt end in 1754, with the death of Carvajal. A few months later, Ensenada was driven from office by Ricardo Wall, the Spanish cavalry officer of Irish descent and future prime minister of Spain, who became Fernando vi's most powerful advisor.

It was the death in August 1758 of Fernando's devoted wife Barbara, the woman who always remained steadfastly by his side, aloof from palace manoeuvring, that broke the monarch's spirit. From the time of her death to that of the king himself exactly a year later, Fernando sank into a state of prostration. There were days when he refused to dress, wandering in his nightgown, unshaven and unwashed, about the gardens facing the Buen Retiro Palace. At other times the king would sit motionless on a stool for hours. Since the couple was childless, when Fernando vi died, he was succeeded by his half-brother Carlos iii, who would be the first monarch to take up residence in the newly completed Royal Palace.

For the nearly three decades in which Carlos iii sat on the throne, Madrid experienced a major boost to its programme of urban reform. A network of roads leading out of the capital from the Puerta del Sol was constructed on his orders. As a tribute, an equestrian statue of the king stands in the middle of the square. It was inspired by a contemporary eighteenth-century wood and plaster sculpture by Juan Pascual de Mena, which can now be seen at the Royal Academy of San Fernando. The modern bronze replica was only put in place in 1994.

Carlos iii could also take credit for the installation of street lighting and the inauguration of a house-numbering system. A corps of inspectors was raised to ensure public footpaths were kept reasonably tidy – a daunting task for a city in which more than five hundred taverns, wine shops and alcohol-serving cafés drew out Madrid's 200,000 citizens to spend long hours in the streets. New sanitation

Carlos III, engraving after a portrait by Goya from 1788.

regulations allowed inspectors to pay weekly visits to homes and levy fines on offenders who failed to keep bins in their courtyards. Tossing rubbish, including human waste, from the window at night was a widespread practice. Home owners were also obliged to install rooftop guttering to prevent rainwater from cascading to the street, with the consequent flooding of building entrances and adjacent footpaths.

One Goya portrait of Carlos III is held in the Bank of Spain collection and another is in the Prado Museum. Both portray the king as a smiling, avuncular man, devoid of any trace of royal haughtiness. It is this manifest kindliness that endeared him to Madrileños, who conferred on their monarch the unofficial title of 'king-mayor'.

The king's determination to embellish and enhance his capital is represented in the Puerta de Alcalá gate that rises imposingly in the Plaza de la Independencia, in the middle of the road that once connected Madrid to Cervantes' birthplace of Alcalá de Henares.

Carlos commissioned his favoured architect, Francesco Sabatini, to build what was to be Europe's first triumphal arch, pre-dating both the Arc de Triomphe in Paris and the Brandenburg Gate in Berlin. Inaugurated in 1778, the arch has sustained war damage on numerous occasions, from the Napoleonic invasion of 1808 to the Spanish Civil War of 1936–9. In both conflicts the arch was peppered with artillery shells, leaving pockmarks in the masonry that are still visible today. A curious architectural feature is the arch's asymmetrical facades. The east face is supported by ten Corinthian columns, while the opposite side, facing downhill towards the Plaza de Cibeles, has two columns flanking the central arch and six rectangular pilasters projecting from the facade. Moreover, the east-facing cornice is crowned by cherubs wielding arms. Those atop the west face wear helmets and are crouched behind banners and shields. The explanation for the disparity is that Sabatini submitted two different plans to Carlos III, who was so taken by the project that he commissioned both designs. The eighteenth-century British physician and geologist Joseph Townsend travelled to Madrid in 1786, a trip that produced his three-volume account *A Journey Through Spain in the Years 1786 and 1787* (published 1791). Townsend was impressed by the Neoclassical Puerta de Alcalá, which he accurately measured as being 'seventy feet high, and the two lateral ones [arches] are thirty-four, all well-proportioned. It is by [Francesco] Sabatini and does credit to his taste.'

The Prado Museum is widely acclaimed as Madrid's Neoclassical magnum opus and its art collection ranks among the finest in the world. The gallery has been praised as one of Europe's crowning glories by foreign visitors, from the Victorian traveller and writer Lady Elizabeth Herbert and Russian revolutionary Leon Trotsky, to the Danish author Hans Christian Andersen and the French Impressionist painter Édouard Manet. It was Manet, in a letter sent in 1865 to his friend Henri Fantin-Latour, who praised the glories of the Prado and in particular the works of Velázquez thus: 'Oh, what a pity you are not here,' he wrote. 'What pleasure it would have given you to see Velázquez, who alone is worth the whole journey.' Curiously, Manet reserved his greatest praise for Velázquez's

The Puerta de Alcalá.

portrait of Felipe IV. How odd the French Impressionist should almost dismiss Velázquez's *Las Meninas* as merely 'another extraordinary picture'. But of course, one must remember that the servant who saved the canvas from the flames of the Royal Alcázar in 1734 did so only because it was one of the few that had not been destroyed by fire, not because of his artistic expertise.

In 1775 Carlos III charged the engineer José de Hermosilla with the task of designing a tree-lined boulevard along a route that became the Paseo del Prado. The architect Ventura Rodríguez added three decorative fountains depicting figures from Greek mythology: Cybele in the Plaza de Cibeles, Apollo midway along and Neptune at the bottom, facing the Botanic Garden. Most celebrated of all the fountains is Cybele, a goddess of great mystery, arriving in a carriage drawn by lions to show her mastery over nature. She is associated with wild music, wine and an ecstatic, disorderly following focused on fertility rites. Although associated with mountains and wilderness, she was also seen as a protector of cities, because she has power over nature that would otherwise threaten the existence of the city and settled, civilized life. The Cibeles fountain was created in 1782, with the goddess and her lions carved in marble and the rest of the fountain in stone. It was mostly sculpted by Francisco Gutiérrez, with the lions being made by the French sculptor Roberto Michel. As well as providing high decorative style to the plaza it was also originally a practical source of water for citizens, with two stand-pipes in operation until 1862 – one for the official water carriers and one for the general public – while the fountain's basin was used as a horse trough. The Cibeles fountain survived the bombardment of the Civil War unscathed, having been covered in sandbags for the duration of the conflict. The statue stands among the foremost symbols of Madrid and is loved as an old friend by Madrileños.

The avenue with its fountains was hailed by the nineteenth-century French writer Théophile Gautier as 'one of the most beautiful promenades in the world'. The *pièce de resistance* of this avenue is one of the outstanding accomplishments of European Neoclassicism, found to the south of the Neptune fountain. The Prado Museum was originally conceived by the king in 1785, three years before his death, as a museum of natural sciences. It was not until 1819 that Carlos's grandson Fernando VII, in one of his more benign moments, and with the encouragement of his wife María Isabel de Braganza, had it adapted to house the royal collection of paintings.

The Cibeles fountain, one of the most symbolic landmarks of Madrid.

Beloved as he was by Madrileños, not all was a bed of roses for Carlos III during his reign. A plaque displayed in the Plaza de Antón Martín, in the Barrio de las Letras, commemorates the Esquilache riots that broke out on this spot on Palm Sunday, 23 March 1766. A Goya canvas held in a private collection in Paris depicts a mob rampaging in the square around the Franciscan monk Father Yecla, who took the people's petition to the palace, preaching from a pedestal. The painting is titled *El motín de Esquilache*, after the king's hugely unpopular chief minister. The people of Madrid had been nursing a grudge against the Marquis of Esquilache ever since his liberalization of the grain trade had brought a sharp rise in food prices. The situation reached breaking point when Esquilache slapped a ban on the wearing of the popular wide-brimmed hat and flowing cape, which most men wore at the time. The minister alleged this attire provided a cover for criminals, from pickpockets to assassins. His plan was to have it replaced with the more 'European' French version of short cape and three-cornered hat. That scheme literally blew up in his face and, by association, reflected badly on the king. Faced with the threat of an attack on the palace, two days after the rebellion began Carlos retired with his family to the Aranjuez royal residence 43 kilometres (27 mi.) to the south of the capital. The king had Esquilache sacked and packed off to Venice as ambassador of the Spanish crown. Carlos appointed the Count of Aranda chief minister, a position invested with all the powers of prime minister. Aranda re-established order in the streets and even managed to persuade the people to adopt the new-style cape and hat, using the argument that the former dress was worn by the public executioner. Calm was finally restored when Carlos issued a letter to his subjects promising to listen to their demands.

One bitterly cold December morning in 1788, a report from the Royal Palace confirmed the king's death. The court physicians had spared no effort to save his life. In a final act of despair, they placed by the dying king's bedside the remains of Madrid's patron saint San Isidro and his wife Santa María de la Cabeza, in the hope that a divine miracle might intercede to spare his life. This tradition of using religious relics for medicinal purposes survived in Spain for nearly two hundred years after. In 1975, with General Franco lying at death's door, his desperate team of doctors sent for the mummified arm of Saint Theresa, which was laid next to the Caudillo in his final hours. Franco had seized this relic from the Church of La Merced in Ronda in 1937. The dictator's life-support machine was switched off shortly afterward and the saint's arm was returned to its rightful resting place.

As far as the people of Madrid were concerned, Carlos III, the king-mayor, would always remain a much-loved ruler. No sooner had the news of his death been made public than tens of thousands of people turned out, from every part of the city, to march in a silent procession in front of the palace.

Statue of Luis Daoíz and Pedro Velarde in the Plaza del Dos de Mayo.

4 Bourbon Farewell – and Return

With the exception of Goya's official court paintings of Carlos IV, little recognition was given to the inept son of the king-mayor. That said, the portraits have a not-too-subtle satirical quality about them, in their rendering of a vacuous royal face set on a bloated torso. A painting held in the Prado Museum's collection of a family gathering, in which Goya included himself in the background, brings to mind Velázquez's self-portrait in *Las Meninas*. The difference is that Felipe v's court painter would never have dared to depict the queen as a grotesque harpy, as did Goya with Carlos's wife María Luisa de Parma. There is evidence to suggest that Goya held the new monarch in comparatively low regard. Several of the early portraits were turned out in obvious haste, especially those that had been commissioned to commemorate Carlos IV's proclamation of ascension in January 1789. These were for the most part produced by his workshop disciples.

It is worth paying a visit to Goya's burial site in San Antonio de la Florida chapel, west of the city centre, by the banks of the Manzanares, to admire the magnificent frescoes he painted on the dome. The architecture's sober appearance contrasts sharply with this grandiose collection of frescoes, painted at the end of the eighteenth century, which portray the chapel's patron St Anthony of Padua. It took Goya four months to complete the ensemble, from painting the angels and ecclesiastical symbols on the spandrels to covering the entire dome with a scene of St Anthony raising a murdered man to life. This depiction of the miracle was set by Goya behind a fictive balcony, around which the artist painted a crowd of his contemporary Madrileños, giving an accurate cross-section of society. When Goya died in 1828, he was buried in France, and sixty years later his remains (minus his mysteriously missing head) were exhumed and sent to Spain. In 1919 he was laid to rest in the tomb in San Antonio de la Florida.

The chapel of San Antonio de la Florida is also symbolic of Carlos IV's role as caretaker monarch. The original shrine to St Anthony was erected in 1770 on the orders of Carlos III. It was later demolished when his son decided to extend the surrounding gardens through the spot occupied by the sanctuary. Carlos IV is often erroneously credited as the chapel's founder, yet all he achieved was to have it rebuilt in a nearby field. In essence, the king did little apart from completing a number of works undertaken by his predecessor. The construction and renovation schemes that had gathered momentum under Carlos III were taken forward by his successor, and this saved Carlos IV from falling into total disrepute in the eyes of Madrid's citizens. The monarch can claim credit for several projects, one of the most prominent being the monumental Fábrica de Tabacos (Tobacco Factory), today a cultural centre in Calle de Embajadores in the heart of the Lavapiés working-class district. The Depósito Hidrográfico (Maritime Archive) in Calle de Alcalá was also initiated under Carlos III and completed by his son. Likewise, the ducal Palacio de Liria, home of the Alba family; the Palacio de Buenavista, now Army Headquarters in Plaza de Cibeles; the Palacio de Villahermosa, a stately home and former bank that in 1992 became the Thyssen-Bornemisza Museum, with its world-class collection spanning eight centuries of European painting; alongside a scattering of churches and stately homes, which were given their finishing touches during Carlos IV's reign.

From a historical perspective, the most significant act of Carlos IV's time on the throne was the appointment of Manuel Godoy to serve as chief minister. This inspiration originated with the king's officious wife, María Luisa, who had cast a covetous eye over this handsome 25-year-old cavalry officer. The ensuing love affair, which the queen referred to in private as 'the earthly trinity', was a much-discussed topic in Madrid, from the refined salons of the nobility

Goya frescoes in the chapel of San Antonio de la Florida.

to the squalid taverns around the Plaza Mayor. This extra-marital relationship served to further discredit a monarch who had indulged his zest for hunting while his navy was being destroyed by the British in the Battle of Trafalgar. Madrid's nobility was also infuriated over the title of 'Prince of Peace' that Carlos had awarded to his scheming minister. As an added affront, Godoy was given a carriage bearing his own monogram.

Godoy ended up the victim of his own unbridled ambition when trouble flared up with Napoleonic France. At Godoy's insistence and with Carlos's blessing, in 1808 the French emperor sent an army into Spain, ostensibly to take control of Portugal, which had been partitioned between both countries, with Godoy as titular ruler of the southern sector. Both the monarch and Godoy had tragically misread Napoleon's intentions: by March of that year Madrid had become a city under French occupation. Sensing the people's growing outrage, Carlos, María Luisa and Godoy thought it prudent to put some distance between themselves and the capital's furious citizens. They fled south to Aranjuez, there to be met by a mob that had travelled from Madrid to besiege the royal family in the Aranjuez palace. There were scenes of widespread rioting – Godoy went into hiding for two days in a rolled-up carpet – before Carlos threw in the towel, abdicating in favour of his son Fernando VII. Relations were always strained between father and son. On one occasion Carlos had Fernando arrested on suspicion of conspiring to secure support from Napoleon to overthrow himself and Godoy, though this was never substantiated. But the king later forgave him.

Carlos IV has been accused of a plethora of character flaws, from witlessness and indolence to outright incompetence. One of the few charges that was not laid against him was wickedness. That sobriquet was reserved for Fernando VII, the most vilified monarch ever to sit on the Spanish throne, and who for a time ironically bore the nickname of 'the Desired', later to be more correctly rechristened 'the Felon'. Shortly after his father's abdication, the 24-year-old Fernando marched triumphantly from Aranjuez to Madrid, arriving on 19 March 1808 to be crowned king. On approaching the Royal Palace, he discovered that a French army had taken possession of the capital the day before. There then ensued an almost surreal episode in European royal history. Napoleon refused to recognize Fernando's claim to the throne. The emperor summoned the entire royal family, Godoy included, to Bayonne. At their first encounter Napoleon took an instant dislike to Fernando, whom he considered a dim and iniquitous man. On 6 May Carlos, encouraged by the queen and Godoy, gave over to the emperor all his rights to the throne in exchange for a pension of 7.5 million francs per annum. Fernando also renounced his hereditary rights for a more modest annuity of 1 million francs. Napoleon was playing a shrewd game: by offering himself as mediator between father and son, he succeeded in drawing them into a trap, allowing him to plunder them both.

The initial agreement was that the crown was to revert to its former holder, only it didn't. No sooner had Carlos been reconfirmed as monarch, the French emperor ordered him to relinquish his title in favour of Napoleon's brother, who for the next five years would rule as Joseph I of Spain. Fernando was sent into gilded retirement, to spend the next six years at the Château de Valençay in the Loire Valley. The king and queen, along with Godoy, were also packed off to France, where María Luisa died in January 1819, followed by Carlos a fortnight later. Godoy soldiered on for another thirty years, living in Italy and France, until his death in Paris in 1851 at the ripe old age of 84.

In having his brother crowned king of Spain, Napoleon had seriously underestimated the degree of opposition he would meet. Instead of a peaceful transition to a Bonaparte monarch, the emperor's gamble led to a full-blown military and political disaster. Madrid lived its finest hour in the weeks that followed Napoleon's invasion and occupation of the city. Its popular uprising against an all-powerful regular army gave Europe its first taste of guerrilla warfare – the term 'guerrilla' is the diminutive of the Spanish *guerra* (war). On 2 May 1808, early in the morning, 2,000 angry Madrileños gathered outside the Royal Palace. The palace's master locksmith had raised the alarm that the royal family was being marched off by the French. The Grenadier Guards outside the palace were taken by surprise and, at some point, the order was given to open fire with muskets and artillery on the protestors. Within minutes, the grounds outside the gates were littered with dead and wounded from both sides. By nine o'clock, a full-scale insurrection was underway.

The Malasaña district near the Gran Vía is known for its hip culture and trendy bars. More than two centuries ago, it was the site of the Monteleón artillery barracks. On 2 May 1808 the small contingent of Spanish troops garrisoned in the army camp dragged their cannons outside to confront the French. The insurrectionists managed to hold out for only an hour against an overwhelming number of enemy soldiers, but those sixty minutes bequeathed to Madrid some of its most illustrious heroes. On the morning of the army insurrection, a group of women rushed out of their homes to fight alongside the Spanish soldiers. One of these women was captured and placed against a wall and shot by French grenadiers. This was Manuela Malasaña, whose name was given to the neighbourhood of her birth. The two leaders of the army rebellion were the artillery officers Luis Daoíz and Pedro Velarde, who manned the

Plaza del Dos de Mayo

In the heart of Madrid's Malasaña district, a trendy area filled with cafés, bakeries and vintage clothing shops, stands the Plaza del Dos de Mayo, with its brick and marble monument to the heroes of the 2 May 1808 uprising against Napoleon's army of occupation. On the morning of the uprising a throng of Madrileños stormed the artillery park demanding weapons for the people. Foremost among these was the fifteen-year-old seamstress Manuela Malasaña, who lived in Calle de San Andrés – today ironically the home of Café Pepe Botella, the nickname of Napoleon's despised brother who was imposed as king, inciting the people to revolt. Wrestled to the ground by French grenadiers, Manuela struggled to fight off her attackers with her sewing scissors. This was her fatal undoing, for the orders were to execute anyone found carrying a weapon. Manuela stood in defiance when she was placed in front of a firing squad. Later that day, an officer delivered the clothes she wore to her family – a cotton blouse and waistcoat, black trousers and felt hat. Manuela's rebellious spirit has stamped itself on the city's history, for let it not be forgotten that the anti-austerity 'Indignados' movement that swept across the world in 2011 began in Madrid, precisely in the month of May.

Eugenio Álvarez Dumont, *Malasaña and his Daughter Fight Against the French, 2 May 1808*, 1887, oil on canvas.

cannons and were both killed in the exchange of fire. The Valencian artist Joaquín Sorolla immortalized Velarde's final moments in his dramatic painting *The Defence of the Monteleón Barracks* (painted 1808–14). Statues of Velarde and Daoíz stand under the small arch in the square, and every year on 2 May, which is a Madrid public holiday, festivities are held around the Plaza del Dos de Mayo to mark the uprising.

With the military rebellion crushed, the French troops made their way south to the Puerta del Sol, where the populace was venting its fury on Napoleon's mounted Mamelukes of the Imperial Guard. The fact that these were Muslim mercenaries served to incite all the more rage, for the episode of nearly eight hundred years of Moorish domination is easily brought to the surface of a Spaniard's thoughts. The butchery that took place that afternoon is immortalized in Goya's *Dos de Mayo* painting in the Prado Museum, along with Goya's *Tres de Mayo* (both painted 1814), which depicts the gruesome execution of Spanish partisans that took place the next night. The rebellion had cost the lives of more than four hundred Madrileños, and those two

Francisco de Goya, *El dos de Mayo de 1808 en Madrid* (also known as *The Charge of the Mamelukes*), 1814, oil on canvas.

Goya, *El tres de mayo de 1808 en Madrid*, 1814, oil on canvas.

days of fighting and the brutal reprisals went down in history as the broadest popular uprising in Europe during that era.

Joseph I was known as *Pepe Botella*, Pepe being the Spanish diminutive for José and *botella* the word for 'bottle'. There is today a wine bar bearing the French king's nickname in the Plaza Dos de Mayo. However, the popular image of Joseph I as a heavy drinker cannot be substantiated. In fact, by reliable accounts he was abstemious, and the nickname instead relates to his removal of the heavy taxes on alcohol when he came to power in 1808, which led to the establishment of many *botillerías* (liquor stores). What is undisputed is that Joseph was detested by the populace, to the extent that when the news reached Madrid of the French army's defeat at Bailén, he was forced to flee the city. The decisive Spanish victory at that battle is depicted in José Casado del Alisal's canvas *The Surrender at Bailén* (1864), which hangs in the Prado Museum. Napoleon's older brother never rose above the standing of a puppet monarch. In 1813, at the end of the French disaster in the Peninsular War, Joseph left Spain for good. The Bonaparte regime was totally dependent on the success of Napoleon's military campaigns. Joseph's government had been forcibly imposed and maintained by foreign troops. Given the disastrous outcome of the Peninsular War, it never stood a chance of survival.

The truth is that Joseph was never going to put a foot right, simply by virtue of being a foreign monarch imposed by a foreign power. His brief, chaotic reign was distinguished by an effort to improve the lot of his hostile subjects whose rancour, as it turned out, was rooted in a misconception. One of his first acts as king was to abolish the Inquisition. Shortly thereafter he restored the bull-fight, which had sunk into disfavour with the Bourbons, to its former glory. Bullfighting had finally been banned by Carlos iv in 1805. Two professional fights were organized to mark Joseph's arrival in Madrid in 1808 and the *corridas* resumed properly from 1810. Joseph also authorized all-night opening hours for Madrid's hundreds of taverns and wine shops, and for the less affluent segment of the population he made free theatre performances available to the working classes. All well and good, until Joseph's modernization designs ran into trouble. The French monarch was shocked by his first encounter with a cluttered and dilapidated Madrid. The Bourbons had directed their efforts to erecting monumental icons like the Royal Palace, while ignoring the tumbledown and insalubrious state of the inner city. Joseph resolved to open up new spaces in the city, but to do so it was necessary to raze a number of religious buildings and residential dwellings that had fallen into a woeful state of disrepair. He took a determined hand to the many churches and convents that had been left unrenovated for centuries and were now dilapidated. One unfortunate victim of the demolition works was Diego Velázquez, more precisely the painter's remains, which lay in the crypt of the Church of San Juan. This was one of Madrid's oldest Christian shrines and dated from the city's Roman occupation. Velázquez and his grave-stone were lost in the rubble, never to be seen again. The church was in the Plaza de Ramales, just south of the Royal Palace. The foundations were exposed during the construction of an underground car park in 2000. A team of archaeologists was brought in but failed to

Cross commemorating Velázquez on the Plaza de Ramales.

turn up any sign of the sarcophagus. A column in the square now marks the spot of Velázquez's burial.

Over the course of several months numerous churches, seven convents and dozens of rickety, structurally unsafe buildings were torn down. In their place, Madrid gained new open spaces and landscaped gardens. The Santa Ana convent gave way to the tree-lined square of the same name, now a children's playground with groupings of benches and tables ringed by cafés and bistros. The Plaza de Oriente facing the Royal Palace was, in the early nineteenth century, a warren of dirt roads. After its clearing and renovation, the square became a showpiece of vast gardens and later the site of the Royal Opera House. The great square was adorned with statues of Spanish monarchs. These were meant to sit on the palace itself, but the architects decided they were too heavy for the building's rooftop. Other squares dating from this time and still in existence include Plaza de la Cebada, Santa Bárbara, Callao and San Ildefonso. Reflecting on how Madrid profited from these initiatives, it is indeed unfortunate that the king's efforts were denounced almost everywhere as an attack on the Church.

On 18 May 1814 Fernando VII made his heroic return to Madrid. Upon his homecoming from an exile of indolence and vice at Talleyrand's estate in France, the king conferred on his capital the title of 'Ever Heroic', in tribute to the people's 2 May revolt against the French. This was added to Madrid's previous accolades of 'Imperial and Crowned', granted by Emperor Carlos I, and the double honours of 'Ever Noble' and 'Ever Loyal' given to the city by the fifteenth-century king of Castile Enrique IV (the Impotent). Fernando's reception at the city gates can only be described as tumultuous, bordering on frenzied. Hundreds of Madrileños rushed forward to unharness the twelve horses pulling the royal carriage, which they then dragged to the Royal Palace.

Two years before Fernando's return to Madrid, the first official political debate in Spanish history took place in Cádiz where, in 1812, the Cortes (parliament) proclaimed a liberal Constitution that imposed severe restraints on royal power. The deputies voted to limit the authority of the monarchy to a responsive veto, within the framework of a modern bourgeois society that placed political control in the hands of the middle classes. Madrileños might have been wondering why Fernando VII's first decree declared the Cádiz Constitution null and void. They were soon to find out.

Goya's rendering of Fernando, displayed in the Prado Museum, shows him as a bloated, scowling despot robed in garish court dress. It evokes the reign of terror that ensued from his return to Madrid until his death in 1833. When army units rose in revolt in 1823, under the leadership of Colonel Rafael de Riego, the arch-reactionary Fernando sought aid from Louis XVIII. The French king dispatched a force, known as the Hundred Thousand Sons of St Louis, which swiftly occupied Madrid. Riego was arrested and, despite his pleas for clemency, Fernando had him hanged, drawn and quartered for public display in the Plaza de la Cebada in the Barrio de la Latina. The *Hymn to Riego* became the national anthem of the liberal opposition and was also adopted by the First and Second Republics.

Even on his deathbed Fernando was capable of stirring up rancour and future confrontation for his country. In defiance of the Madrid Cortes, which in 1789 had repealed the Salic Law that forbade a female from ascending the throne, Fernando reinstated this ruling, thereby creating an uproar in his wife María Cristina's camp. The law had been enshrined by the Bourbons in 1713, during the War of the Spanish Succession, to prevent the crown falling once again into Habsburg hands. In the end, Fernando acquiesced and withdrew the decree, so that when his three-year-old daughter came of age she would rule as Isabel II, with María Cristina in the meantime acting as regent. No sooner had Fernando breathed his last than the followers of Carlos IV's second surviving son, Don Carlos de Borbón, proclaimed him the rightful ruler. Spain was about to embark on its first civil war in three centuries, a conflict that at one point brought the Carlist armies perilously close to the walls of Madrid.

Characteristic turret in the bourgeois Salamanca district.

5 Madrid Comes of Age

Along with the political tumult of the nineteenth century came the rebirth of a literary tradition that had all but died out in Madrid, especially under Fernando VII's reign, when numerous writers and intellectuals fled into exile. When the infant Isabel was proclaimed queen in 1833 and her mother became regent, Madrid was still basking in the glory of Golden Age immortals who had put the city on the European literary map two hundred years previously. The late eighteenth century produced talented writers, above all playwrights like Leandro Fernández de Moratín and Ramón de la Cruz. None of them, however, could aspire to the greatness of Cervantes, Lope de Vega, Quevedo or Góngora. Cervantes' name remains best-known to followers of classical Spanish literature, but as Mark Williams points out, 'Cervantes was but the brightest of many literary lights during Spain's Golden Age.'

A political development of lasting consequence for Madrid, and which pitched liberals in a furious fight against traditionalists, was the *desamortización de Mendizábal*, the confiscation of Church property ordered in 1835 by María Cristina's anti-clerical prime minister, Juan Álvarez de Mendizábal. The implementation of Mendizábal's decree was greeted with cheers by a sector of the public that suspected the clergy of deliberately spreading an Asian flu epidemic among infidels. In July 1834 some 1,500 cases had been confirmed in some of Madrid's most squalid neighbourhoods. Other conspiracy theorists were convinced that the Carlists had been responsible for introducing the deadly disease into the city. Of course, it is much simpler to pin the blame on a soft target at arm's reach than an elusive enemy without. The soft target in this instance was the clergy, who were driven out of Madrid nearly four decades before the final defeat of the staunchly Catholic Carlist army by liberal forces.

In January 1836 the few priests and nuns left in Madrid were chased out by an angry horde, who over the course of the next six months lent their enthusiastic support to the demolition of thirteen of the capital's most ancient churches and convents. These exiled men and women of God were the lucky ones: in the previous months, many had been murdered in the streets by anti-clerical rioters. The Carlist enemy would, of course, denounce this as an act of unspeakable sacrilege, and many members of Madrid's nobility and traditionalists uttered agreement, albeit in quiet voices. But was the confiscation really an act of political vandalism? The *cronista de la villa* (official Madrid historian) Federico Carlos Sainz de Robles (1898–1983) drew attention to what came to replace the razed churches in the years following Mendizábal's pronouncement: a number of small squares, modern military barracks, public works schemes, charity hostels, markets and other projects of indisputable benefit to the people of Madrid. In some instances, property belonging to the Church was replaced by government institutions. This was the case with the Espíritu Santo Convent in Carrera de San Jerónimo, which became the site of the Chamber of Deputies. The Augustin Order María de Aragón Convent in Plaza de la Marina became the Senate house. The Jesuit novitiate in Calle de San Bernardo was taken over to serve as the Universidad Central, until the new sprawling campus was built beyond the Moncloa arch on the city's western outskirts.

The government's seizure and demolition of religious buildings was a radical and highly controversial act. Nevertheless, it contributed to the modernization of Madrid and helped to transform it from a city dominated by ecclesiastical structures to one with taller, more salubrious buildings and new open spaces, befitting the capital's embryonic middle class. The mainspring behind Madrid's rebirth of the nineteenth century was the city's mayor, Joaquín Vizcaíno, Marquis of Pontejos. A century after the Marquis of Vadillo, another reformist nobleman who occupied what was to become the office of mayor, had founded the Cuartel del Conde Duque, Vizcaíno implemented a series of far-reaching changes of his own in the city's infrastructure. In his brief two-year tenure, from 1834 to 1836, Vizcaíno banned hawkers from public squares – a practice that has returned with a vengeance, with scores of touts selling knock-off fashion items along the Gran Vía and other main shopping streets. They are known as *manteros*, or 'blanketeers', for their system of swiftly scooping up their goods in a blanket and scarpering at the first sign of police. Another of Vizcaíno's efforts to endow the city with a more modern appearance was the introduction of a house-numbering system, even ones on the right and odd on the left side of all roads, starting from the end closest to the Puerta del Sol. Streets signs were put up on corner buildings; oil lamps were installed in main thoroughfares (gas lamps were introduced in 1848); pavements were raised above road level to protect pedestrians from carriages and splashing mud; a system of regular rubbish collection was started, using sealed bins on donkey carts; the San Bernardino alms house was opened; paving stones were replaced in damaged roads, which with a certain twist of irony were hailed as 'Royal Pontejos Ways'; a 24-hour fire alarm system was put into operation; the first savings bank was inaugurated; a corps of *serenos*, or night watchmen, was recruited; and thousands of trees were planted throughout the city.

The game-changer in urban development was the advent of the Barrio de Salamanca. This new neighbourhood, which can be likened to the eighth arrondissement in Paris, extended Madrid north and east, starting from the Retiro Park to the south and Paseo de la Castellana as the western border. The Marquis of Salamanca, after whom the neighbourhood is named, identified the need to build a new district in which Madrid's new bourgeoisie could lead a comfortable, uncluttered life, fleeing the narrow and insalubrious streets of the historic centre.

A decade before her abdication in 1870, Isabel II put her seal of approval on the 'Plan Castro', a scheme drawn up by her liberal-minded public works minister Claudio Moyano. This was an ambitious plan to demolish what was left of Felipe IV's walls and

Greetings card with an illustration of a *sereno* (night watchman).

Serenos

In the dead of night, the calm of a Madrid residential street shatters with a clapping of hands and a cry of *¡Sereno!* Almost immediately, from somewhere nearby comes the echoing reply, *¡Voy!* (On my way!). In a matter of moments, an individual in a greatcoat and peaked cap appears trotting along the street, jangling a ring of heavy and unwieldy brass keys of medieval appearance on his belt. When the *sereno* reaches the caller's heavy wrought-iron gate, the conversation is mostly limited to '*Buenas noches, Sr González*', followed by '*Buenas noches, Pepe.*' The *sereno* produces a key and wishes you a good night's sleep, as you place a five-peseta coin in his hand. *Serenos* were salaried municipal employees until the 1960s, when it was decided to replace their wages with a system of tips. It speaks volumes of city salaries of the time that on average this boosted their income tenfold. The earliest references to Madrid's corps of *serenos* dates from 1765, when night watchmen patrolled the streets, lighting the city's street lamps and keeping a watchful eye for burglars and muggers. Their job was to announce the hour and weather: for instance, *Las doce y todo sereno* (Twelve o'clock and calm), or *La una y lloviendo* (One o'clock and raining). In the twentieth century, the *serenos*' remit was broadened to include the job of gatekeeper, since Madrileños were loath to carry a heavy key to the building when going out for the evening. The *serenos* started their night shift at midnight in summer and an hour earlier in winter, and they were expected to remain on duty until dawn. This venerable institution came to an end in the late 1970s, when locks on most front doors were changed to take modern keys.

create a new residential neighbourhood for the city's emergent bourgeoisie. One of Spain's wealthiest businessmen, José Salamanca y Mayol, the Marquis of Salamanca, put his fortune behind the project, nearly leaving himself bankrupt. He ultimately had to sell his grand stately home in the Paseo de Recoletos, which is now part of the bank BBVA and is used as an exhibition centre. But Salamanca's name remains enshrined in Madrid's most wealthy and stylish barrio, an area on a par with the fashionable neighbourhoods of any European capital.

The Carlist offensive on Madrid in 1837 ended in a rout for the attacking forces, with the pretender Don Carlos and thousands of his followers fleeing to France and the subsequent proclamation of Isabel as the legitimate queen. Madrileños could take solace in the fact that the threat from without had been eliminated. Three years later, they would have to confront the threat from within.

The Calle de Esparteros comes to an end a few yards from the Puerta del Sol. The name of this revolutionary soldier is an appropriate one for a street that almost connects with the stage for Madrid's political and social upheavals. An equestrian statue of General Baldomero Espartero stands just beyond the Plaza de la Independencia. It was erected in 1886, in the middle of what is now the six-lane Calle de Alcalá, hardly noticed by motorists whose attention is fixed on keeping up with the surge of traffic in one of Madrid's busiest roadways. In 1840 the progressive Espartero was the most hotly debated character in Madrid's bourgeoning *tertulia* cafés. In that year, the hero who had defeated the Carlists forced María Cristina to step down as regent and took the title upon himself, virtually making himself dictator.

Espartero's regency lasted but two years, during which time Madrid found itself immersed in a bitter tug-of-war between reformist liberals and moderate conservatives. At the same time, the clergy was pushed to the right by the wave of confiscations and sell-offs of Church property. Government hostility towards the Church was to manifest nearly a century later, when the Church hierarchy threw in its lot with the 1936 military coup that plunged Spain into civil war. In 1843 Espartero was ousted from office by the army's

Queen Isabel II
towards the
end of her
reign, c. 1868.

moderate faction after a skirmish fought outside Madrid. This time,
the people were not on the dictator's side: Madrid erupted in a widespread protest that drove him from office and into exile in England.
Espartero's downfall was consolidated when the thirteen-year-old
Isabel was proclaimed queen later that year, in a magnificent ceremony watched by a jubilant multitude outside the Royal Palace. Her
reign signalled the start of a quarter-century of palace intrigues and
barracks conspiracies, a relentless battle of moderate and liberal factions against progressives, that sowed the seeds for the Revolution
of 1868. Madrid had for years, if not decades, been caught up in a
wave of almost ceaseless instability, but this did not bring to a halt a
host of improvements in the city's social and cultural life. The Naval
Museum in the Paseo del Prado; the Teatro de la Zarzuela off the
Calle de Alcalá; the opening of the Mediodía station, Madrid's first
railway station, that was to become Atocha – these were a few of
the enhancements brought about during and between Espartero's
years in office. These years also ushered in a literary renaissance

Novelist Benito Pérez Galdós at a *tertulia* in 1897.

in Madrid and the advent of cafés, which became the forum for the city's famed *tertulias*, or literary and political debates. This was the Age of Romanticism, in which nineteenth-century writers from across Spain who wished to make their mark were drawn to Madrid like pins to a magnet. The poet José de Espronceda moved to the capital from Extremadura; José Zorrilla, the creator of *Don Juan Tenorio*, was a native of Valladolid; the playwright Gustavo Adolfo Bécquer was an Andalusian from Seville; the dramatist Bretón de los Herreros came from La Rioja.

Madrid embraced the rise of café society, which became the platform for debates among the rival factions. Writers, artists and politicians in search of a lively spot to give vent to their opinions were spoilt for choice. Gradually, the capital became home to 65 thriving cafés, to serve a population of some 300,000. The predecessor to this upsurge in *tertulia* cafés was La Fontana de Oro, in Calle de la Victoria. It was immortalized by the early twentieth-century writer Benito Pérez Galdós, who set the action of his novel *La fontana de oro* in this café during the so-called Liberal Triennium of 1820–23, when a liberal government ruled in Madrid. This once majestic rendezvous for thinkers and literary elites has now become an Irish pub. The first organized *tertulia* was held in the Fonda de San Sebastián, a former inn in the Barrio de las Letras. This became a sanctuary for writers of the Romantic school, like the dramatist Leandro Fernández de Moratín, whose father Nicolás had presided over the café's debut *tertulia*. The *tertulia* can trace its origins back to the *mentideros,* which got their start in the days of Cervantes and Lope de Vega. This was a kind of oral journalism, or street corner forum, in which Madrileños gathered to exchange gossip and catch up on the news of the day. The most traditional *mentidero* was in Calle del León in the Barrio de las Letras, frequented mainly by writers and stage actors. Others were set up in the Puerta del Sol, Calle Mayor and in the environs of the Alcázar. The public would stroll from one *mentidero* to another, to hear the latest palace rumours,

Benito Pérez Galdós, immortalized in tiles on the facade of the café 'El Parnasillo del Principe'.

news from the American colonies and what was on offer in the city's outdoor theatres.

Only two establishments can today lay claim to being direct descendants of Madrid's *tertulia* cafés. The oldest of these is the Café Comercial in the Glorieta de Bilbao. Founded in 1887, this masterful Art Deco work of marble and mirrors is still staffed by waiters wearing the traditional white jacket and black bow-tie. The home of the *tertulia* incarnate is the Café Gijón in the Paseo de Recoletos. It opened a year after the Comercial, in Madrid's café heyday, and still attracts groups of poets and journalists to nightly discussions. Being a waiter in Madrid is not a job – it is a profession. Nowhere is this professionalism more in evidence than at the Café Gijón, the last survivor of Madrid's nineteenth-century literary cafés. José Bárcena has been serving coffee and drinks at the Gijón for more than a third of its 130-year history. He is revered as an institution, for he is the person responsible for organizing *tertulias*. On Mondays Bárcena can be found taking orders from a table of poets, all vociferously proclaiming the glories of their lyrical endeavours. On other days he is to be found discussing politics and literature on an equal footing with writers and academics at their *tertulia* tables. The Gijón is a great social equalizer, the café in which Bárcena contemplates with equal nostalgia the portraits of Nobel Laureate Camilo José Cela and humble Alfonso, the café's much-mourned cigarette vendor, both of whom were personal acquaintances of this venerable waiter.

Writer Elizabeth Nash was impressed by these two cafés' exuberant, almost deafening environments: 'There are nights when you can hardly find a seat at the Gijón or the Comercial and you must struggle to make yourself heard. These traditional haunts seem to have embedded themselves into the city's social milieu, earning themselves a sort of spiritual heritage protection, as well as attracting new fans.'

In 1854 Isabel II called on Espartero to support her tottering throne. Rising to the occasion, the so-called 'Prince of Peace' forced his way back into power in what was virtually a *coup d'état*. He ruled as prime minister for a further two years, with the support of the progressives, until 1856 when he resigned in disgust over constant feuding with fellow army officers, particularly General Leopoldo O'Donnell. Again the people turned against their former hero. Widespread rioting broke out in the streets as mobs ransacked and, in some cases, torched the homes of government ministers and the nobility. Barricades were erected around the Puerta del Sol, the time-honoured rallying point for insurrections. The worst case of violence was the murder of the city's police chief, who was dragged from his home and shot in the Plaza de la Cebada. Coming on the heels of these disturbances, in 1865 a large body of students was whisked off to prison for protesting the dismissal of the popular professor Emilio Castelar, who had condemned the queen's order to sell off some state property. Three years later a *pronunciamiento* by military leaders put a progressive government in power, while Isabel II was away on holiday. The students who had been imprisoned ran through the streets, tearing down all royal emblems they could find in their path.

Madrid now tumbled headlong into a protracted cycle of political turbulence, coups and counter-coups. For Isabel, the writing was on the wall. The queen was forced to abdicate when troops loyal

Mid-19th-century allegorical drawing with typical Madrid characters outside the Café Suizo, with a poster proclaiming the Republic.

to her were defeated by an army of republican forces in what has come to be known as the Glorious Revolution. The so-called 'revolution' came about in the wake of a confrontation between two army generals: the founder of the Liberal Union, Leopoldo O'Donnell, and his arch-enemy in the ranks, Ramón María Narváez, leader of the Moderate Party. O'Donnell clashed with the queen over her demands for drastic measures against those who sought to overthrow the monarchy, and he finally chose to exile himself in Biarritz. Narváez was called on to head the government, but his death in 1868 opened the way for republican forces to rise against the queen. Two years later, the forty-year-old Isabel left for exile in France and in her stead, the provisional government appointed the second son of Victor Emmanuel II of Italy, to rule as Amadeo I. By his own admission, Amadeo was unable to cope with the political mayhem of Madrid and abdicated three years after ascending the throne, dismissing the Spanish people as ungovernable. Spain's First Republic was proclaimed that same night, to an outpouring of jubilation in the Puerta del Sol. The downfall of the republican

Monument to Alfonso XII alongside the boating lake in Retiro Park.

Engraving of an early tram in the Puerta del Sol.

government came a year later in 1874, when monarchist General Arsenio Martínez Campos issued a *pronunciamiento* that put Isabel's eldest son Alfonso XII on the throne.

One of the great accomplishments of Alfonso XII's eleven-year reign, which ended with his untimely death in 1885, was the construction of the Gothic-revival cathedral of Santa María la Real de Almudena. The original church had been built on a site once occupied by Madrid's first mosque, within the Moorish walls. Construction began in 1879 but was not completed until over a century later, in 1993. It stands now as a memorial to Alfonso's young wife María de las Mercedes, who had died within six months of their marriage. The king himself did not enjoy a long life. When Alfonso died at the age of 28, his second wife María Cristina (not to be confused with Fernando VII's wife of the same name who was regent from 1833 to 1840) ruled as regent for seventeen years until their son, Alfonso XIII, came of age in 1902. According to Spanish historian Pedro Montoliú, 'The declaration of Alfonso XIII's coming of age in May 1902 signalled a new change for the city.'

Alfonso XIII's reign marked a time of technological advance and modernization, exemplified by the introduction of electric trams, the telephone system and the opening of the Madrid stock

Gran Vía in 1913.

exchange, which helped impose order on a free-for-all system of commerce. More than one hundred dirt roads and cobbled streets were asphalted, and the first hydraulic lifts were installed in Madrid's newest buildings. In 1919 Alfonso XIII opened the first Metro line, which covered a 3.2-kilometre (2-mi.) route between the working-class district of Cuatro Caminos and the Puerta del Sol. Madrid's Barajas airport was constructed in 1927, though it wasn't opened to air traffic until April 1931 – the month of the king's downfall.

These were days of sweeping changes in the city's development, and the crowning glory of the innovations was the construction of the Gran Vía. From its earliest days, the street that is now Calle de Alcalá had served as an integral component of Madrid's urban growth. Given its fast-growing population, the city needed to expand eastward, as the Manzanares River and royal lands blocked its spread in other directions. The Paseo de la Castellana allowed for the free flow of traffic north and south. The challenge was to open an east–west route. City Hall planners had their eye on the great thoroughfares of Paris, designed in the 1860s by Baron George-Eugène Haussmann.

The Gran Vía today.

Shortly before the turn of the century, Madrid municipal architects José López Salaberry and Francisco Andrés Octavio Palacios came up with the idea of a near mile-long avenue, starting from Calle de Alcalá, to link Plaza de Cibeles with Plaza de España. Financing for the project was obtained from the French banker Martin Albert Silver. Appropriately enough, it was Silver who, on the morning of 4 April 1910, handed to Alfonso XIII a silver pickaxe, with which the king delivered a robust blow to the facade of the parish house of the Church of San José. This was the first of 358 buildings, including several churches, that were earmarked for demolition over the next nineteen years. The completion of the Gran Vía opened a Pandora's box, for this long avenue was to become one of Madrid's most gridlocked and polluted roads. In 2018 Mayor Manuela Carmena introduced a €6.5 million plan for the partial pedestrianization of the Gran Vía, the first major overhaul in its hundred-year history. At the time of writing, after nine months of work, the new traffic layout trims the flow from six to four lanes: one for buses and taxis and another shared by cars and bicycles on each side of the road. On the section from the Plaza de España to Plaza del Callao, one lane is restricted exclusively to cyclists. In addition, the pavement has been widened for pedestrians. As well as having new traffic lights and 144 street benches, the popular avenue now has 89 ornamental pear trees. This was always going to be a highly controversial scheme, and the months of disruption caused by the works raised the predictable outcry from motorists. But it worked. Madrileños can now stroll along a Gran Vía largely free of choking traffic fumes.

Alfonso XIII's birth in the Royal Palace foreshadowed an outbreak of political strife, such as Madrid had not experienced since the downfall of Isabel II. That year, 1886, had seen a barracks revolt against the monarchy in Madrid. The mutiny was swiftly quashed by General Manuel Pavía, a military leader of ambiguous political leanings. He had participated in the revolution that removed Isabel II from power but had also led the coup that brought down the First Republic, allegedly riding his horse into the Cortes to issue his *pronunciamiento*. Fortunately for Alfonso XIII, on that day the feisty Pavía came out on the side of monarchy.

The king himself was to get a first-hand taste of the violence sweeping the capital. On 30 May 1906, a warning was crudely carved into a tree in the Retiro Park. The message read, 'Alfonso XIII will be executed on his wedding day.' It was signed: 'Unrepentant.' No one had spotted it. The following morning the king married Victoria Eugenia of Battenberg in the Church of Los Jerónimos. After the ceremony, the newly-weds rode to the palace in an open carriage. As they were passing a spot in Calle Mayor, now occupied by the traditional Madrid restaurant Casa Ciriaco, a Catalan anarchist named Mateo Morral hurled a bomb wrapped in a bouquet of flowers from a fourth-storey balcony. One horse was killed and several people were injured in the blast, but the monarchs miraculously escaped unharmed. Six years later, Alfonso was riding on horseback in the Calle de Alcalá, near the Bank of Spain, when another anarchist detonated a bomb in his path. This second assassination attempt also ended in failure, but it was symptomatic of a political situation that was steadily slipping out of the monarch's grasp. These were troubled times for his country. In 1898 Spain had suffered a humiliating defeat in the Spanish–American War and had lost its last colonial possessions, Puerto Rico, Cuba and the Philippines, to the United States. Two of the king's prime ministers were shot dead in the streets of Madrid, José Canalejas in 1912 and Eduardo Dato in 1921. Between 1902 and 1906 Alfonso had to deal with fourteen ministerial crises and eight different prime ministers. The climate of extreme political instability had taken Alfonso's rule to the brink. In a foretaste of things to come, in 1923 the army mounted a coup led by General Miguel Primo de Rivera, father of José Antonio Primo de Rivera, founder of the Falange fascist party. The king was now fully under the wing of the Primo de Rivera dictatorship. Spain now had a system of dictatorial monarchy that blackened the king's name in the eyes of many of his subjects.

In 1929 General Primo de Rivera was given a warning by army commanders, informing the dictator that given the steady escalation of street protests and a landslide republican victory in municipal elections, they were no longer prepared to prop up a tottering monarchy. The general stepped down from power and went into exile in Paris, where he died two months later. There followed a short-lived government, under a less dictatorial but also ineffectual military leader, General Dámaso Berenguer. Finally, in 1931, the military all but withdrew their support for the monarchy, leaving Alfonso XIII no choice but to give up his throne. The morning the king boarded a train for Rome, tens of thousands of Madrileños once more flooded into the Puerta del Sol, this time to celebrate the proclamation of the Second Republic. Spain held its breath.

6 City Under Siege

Madrid has been a battle-seasoned city for nearly a thousand years, from the day in 1085 when the Moors were driven out of their fortification, Magerit, by Alfonso VI of León and Castile. Tumultuous events such as the 2 May 1808 uprising against the French occupation, or the Glorious Revolution of 1868 – both instances which, almost inevitably, had the Puerta del Sol as their backdrop – stand out as two of the most heroic episodes in the city's annals. The venerable square has also been the setting for *pronunci-amientos* by disgruntled army officers, the proclamation of Spain's two Republics and innumerable student and worker protests. This is the city whose people in 2004 stood as one in defiance of the Islamist bombings of the Atocha railway station that left 192 dead and nearly 2,000 injured. Seven years later, in May 2011, Madrid again showed its fighting spirit, when the *Indignados* (Indignant) anti-austerity movement emerged in the Puerta del Sol and rapidly spread to cities around the world.

Never was Madrid's mettle so severely put to the test as in the Spanish Civil War, when the city withstood two and a half years of siege and daily shelling. In those years, 1936 to 1939, Madrid also earned the dubious distinction of being the world's first European capital city to undergo aerial bombardment. The Telefónica building dominates the skyline at the top of the Gran Vía. Completed in 1930, it was one of the last of Madrid's major construction projects inaugurated by King Alfonso XIII. The broad, white-faced building opened its doors as a subsidiary of the U.S. telecoms group International Telephone and Telegraph (ITT), and at the time it was the tallest building in Madrid. The U.S. connection goes beyond that of a commercial relationship. Telefónica's architect was Ignacio de Cárdenas, who designed the building in the New York studio of Louis S. Weeks, the creator of ITT's Manhattan headquarters.

Telefónica today is dwarfed by the 43-storey Torre Picasso tower in one of Madrid's main commercial areas: the AZCA complex that straddles the Paseo de la Castellana. Both buildings were overtaken in 2009 by the 57-storey Torre Espacio, one of the four office blocks in the Cuatro Torres Business Area (CTBA) further north along the same avenue. In 1936 General Franco discovered that, contrary to plans, he was not going to take Madrid by storm and switched his offensive strategy to attempt taking the city by siege. Telefónica immediately became more than a prestigious symbol of Madrid's technological progress – it was now a military target. The top floors of the structure, which gave spectacular views of the front line to the north and west, were used as an observation platform by the Republican military commanders and their Soviet advisors. The building was also a perfect rangefinder for Nationalist gunners positioned on the hillsides of the Casa de Campo. The Gran Vía became known as *Avenida de la muerte* (Death Avenue).

Madrid's 1.3 million inhabitants did their level best to 'keep calm and carry on' during those dark days of the siege. The Metro system was the city's main air-raid shelter, while at the same time continuing to serve passengers. In 1937, at the height of the bombardment, the Metro logged more than 130 million journeys. To take their minds off bombs and hunger, Madrileños flocked by their thousands to the city's 23 cinemas to watch Charlie Chaplin films, Spanish romantic comedies and Soviet propaganda documentaries. The most frequented cinemas were clustered around the Gran Vía, where nowadays they continue to draw in the crowds. Fascist artillery attacks were frequently timed to coincide with the ends of films, when the forces laying siege to Madrid knew the street would be thronged with people. The Cine Rialto, inaugurated in 1930, is now a theatre. The Cine Capitol, also in the Gran Vía,

The Telefónica building stands at the top of the Gran Vía.

People taking refuge in the Metro during the Nationalist bombings, 1937.

opened in October 1933. The undisputed gem is the Cine Callao, an award-winning Art Deco interior shaped like the prow of an ocean liner. The gigantic auditorium has a seating capacity of more than 2,000. The cinema was built in 1926 in the Plaza del Callao, Spain's busiest square, through which more than 113 million people now pass every year.

Franco's forces were supported with personnel and equipment from Nazi Germany, including around 7,000 troops, an estimated 850,000 guns and several squadrons of Luftwaffe fighter planes and bombers. There was no escape from the Luftwaffe's indiscriminate bombing. On a November evening in 1936, the Prado Museum was hit by nine incendiary bombs. The Bellas Artes Academy in Calle de Alcalá and the National Library also took direct hits. The threat of the Prado's eventual destruction, and with it one of the world's greatest art collections, prompted the government to order the evacuation of the museum's most valuable treasures. Hundreds of masterpieces like Velázquez's *Las Meninas* and Goya's 'black paintings' – a series of fourteen murals from his home at Quinta del

Sorda, in the southwestern outskirts of Madrid, painted between 1819 and 1823, and later attached to canvas and moved to the Prado – were packed onto lorries and sent to Valencia. By 1938 this provisional capital was also threatened and the works were moved to Barcelona and again, a year later, to the Geneva headquarters of the League of Nations. The paintings were returned to the Nationalist government six days after Germany invaded Poland and the Second World War began.

The Hotel Florida, clad in a magnificent marble facade, was built in 1924 in Plaza del Callao, a few minutes from the Telefónica building and less than a kilometre from the front line. This landmark establishment, demolished in 1964, served as the nerve centre for foreign war correspondents during the civil war. Frequent guests included renowned personalities like Ernest Hemingway, Martha Gellhorn, John Dos Passos and Antoine de Saint-Exupéry. The rest of the clientele was composed largely of arms dealers, officers on leave and an assortment of prostitutes and other picturesque characters. Hemingway and his colleagues would emerge from the hotel in the evening to telex their magazine and newspaper stories from Telefónica, which served as the headquarters of the Foreign Press Bureau. Their reports had to pass through the censorship bureau,

Hotel Florida postcard, *c.* 1920.

Cervecería Alemana, Plaza de Santa Ana, still open today.

whose head at the time was the writer Arturo Barea, who emigrated to Britain in 1939 where he worked for the BBC Overseas Service (now the World Service), broadcasting a weekly talk for the Spanish-language section.

A daily visit to one or more of Madrid's watering holes became a ritual for foreign journalists, Hemingway foremost among them. They were often joined by soldiers of the International Brigades who fought for the Republic, along with adventure-seekers and a hotch-potch of hangers-on. Many of these favoured bars remain very much in existence today. On many an evening, La Venencia, the iconic sherry bar in Calle de Echegaray, would be host to a pre-dinner influx of foreign correspondents, all crowded around the polished mahogany bar, with the barman marking down their orders on the bar top in white chalk, as is still the custom. The Cervecería Alemana in the Plaza de Santa Ana was another Hemingway haunt. The bar is famed for its beer and tapas, though Hemingway was most likely more attracted by its bullfight decor. This is where he would spend quiet afternoon hours, seated at the window table which the waiters always held for him.

The pre-eminent gathering spot for drinks was Bar Chicote in the Gran Vía. The cocktail lounge was founded in 1931 by Perico Chicote, the former head barman of the Palace Hotel. In a conversation one afternoon, a few years before his death in 1977, Chicote recalled a vivid picture of Hemingway, who was one of his most assiduous customers. He described the novelist as a 'big, back-slapping American who often had difficulty holding his liquor'. Chicote indicated a barstool where Hemingway held court into the late hours, and then pointed to the floor. 'That is where he would frequently end his evening.' Hemingway was one of an illustrious list of celebrities who frequented Bar Chicote. This included politicians from both ends of the spectrum, from the founder of the Falange, José Antonio Primo de Rivera, to the firebrand Communist leader Dolores Ibárruri, known as *La Pasionaria* (Passion Flower), who was celebrated for her wartime slogan *¡No Pasarán!* Ava Gardner, Rita Hayworth, Gregory Peck and Frank Sinatra would stop in for a cocktail in later years when passing through Madrid. So too football stars Alfredo Di Stéfano and Ferenc Puskás, not to overlook figures from the international royalty set, like Prince Rainier of Monaco and Princess Soraya of Iran.

Recently given an Art Deco refit, with the clientele now a less dazzling but equally devoted set of cocktail lovers, Museo Chicote, as it has been renamed, ranks as an integral piece of Madrid's cultural history. The change of name is somewhat ironic, for Chicote had in the 1930s amassed a collection of almost 20,000 rare and exotic drinks from around the world, which he put on display in his downstairs museum. The collection was purchased in the 1980s by José María Ruiz-Mateos, shortly before his failed conglomerate Rumasa was expropriated by the government. The bottles were bought by an anonymous American investor and their whereabouts are unknown, but the collection's original home now bears the name of 'museum'.

When not imbibing at Bar Chicote or embroiled in love affairs at the Hotel Florida, foreign correspondents were dodging shells in the streets along with ordinary Madrileños. One of the less high-profile journalists was Sir Geoffrey Cox, who was filing dispatches to the *News Chronicle* in London. Toledo fell to the Nationalists in September 1936 and Franco, leading his column of legionnaires and Moors, continued the march on Madrid, confident the capital would fall by October. The press throughout the world was running banner headlines proclaiming 'the last hours of Madrid'. Cox was one of the few in the dissenting camp. He says that in the last days of October, 'there were already some signs that the miracle might happen'. He goes on to describe an event that helped make this miracle a reality:

> I was drinking coffee in the bar of the Gran Vía [hotel] when I heard shouting and clapping outside. Up the street from the direction of the Ministry of War came a long column of marching men. The International Column of Anti-Fascists had arrived in Madrid. We were watching the First Brigade of what was to develop into the most truly international army the world has seen since the Crusades.

By November 1936 Franco had to face the hard reality that Madrid was not going to fall into his hands without a fight. That was when he called for bombers from his Nazi allies, along with Spanish aircraft, to begin a protracted attack on civilian targets. Cox highlights the business-as-usual mindset that prevailed in the city during the bombardments:

> Monday in central Madrid. An unexploded six-inch shell sticks half out of the paving stones between the tram rails in Calle Montera [adjacent to the Puerta del Sol]. Two navvies are digging it out with picks. A tram, passing only two feet away, slows down and the driver leans out to take a close look at the shell.

The windows of the tram are white with faces. A newspaper seller on the pavement opposite sits on a box dangling his feet and calling '*El Socialista, El Socialista*'.

Helen Grant worked as an interpreter for a group sent to Madrid by the Society of Friends. One diary entry from April 1937 reveals the near indifference Madrileños had adopted to death raining from the skies, after nearly six months of relentless bombardment. It reads:

> The main impression on walking about Madrid is that nobody even thinks about danger. Nevertheless, the majority of the houses and shops in the Gran Vía have been hit . . . Although the guns roar almost continually and sometimes are quite deafening, no one appears to take any notice.

Madrid was overrun and taken by the Nationalists on 28 March 1939, four days before the capitulation of the Republic brought to a close three years of fratricidal warfare. It is important to highlight the word 'taken', for the city did not formally capitulate. No surrender document was ever signed. Madrid had spent two and a half years locked in a sanguine battle against an overwhelming enemy, but never gave up. The city's stubborn resistance had prolonged the war, a fact that had not escaped the attention of Franco and his generals. The reprisals would be terrible: Madrileños were to be mistrusted and thousands would be put in front of Falangist firing squads. For the victors the city was seen as a Marxist stronghold, whose anti-Fascist convictions would be nurtured behind closed doors. Several of the army hierarchy even proposed moving the capital to Seville, a conservative and more regime-friendly city.

Geoffrey Cox acknowledged early on that Madrid might eventually be captured by the besieging forces. The resistance of a half-starved populace, enduring relentless bombardment day and night from their fascist countrymen, supporting troops and artillery from fascist Italy and Nazi Germany's Luftwaffe, was becoming an increasingly futile struggle for survival. 'Whatever the future brings,'

'They shall not pass!' banner outside the Plaza Mayor, c. 1936–7.

Cox concluded in his account, 'the defence of Madrid remains, in face of the terrible odds, one of the finest chapters in the history of the common people of the world.'

When at last the artillery shells and Luftwaffe bombs stopped falling, Madrid emerged from the war a city shattered in morale, its infrastructure and supply lines of basic necessities in tatters. The capital's vital functions had been short-circuited and they would remain so for almost a decade. It was not until the 1950s that Madrid gradually recovered a semblance of normalcy. This came about thanks to the 1953 aid package agreed with the United States, in exchange for four American bases on Spanish soil. One of these was a U.S. Air Force base just outside the city in Torrejón de Ardoz, now occupied by the Spanish military. The 1959 Stabilization Plan helped to restore order to a situation of uncontrolled growth and speculation that had been set in motion by an inner circle of Franco acolytes. The plan was only made possible in the wake of a brutal power struggle in 1957 in which a group of young technocrats from the Opus Dei Catholic lay organization ousted the group of Franco's Falangist cronies who had been entrenched in the Cabinet since the end of the war. These skilled and ambitious bankers and economists began to open the country's doors to foreign tourism and investment. As a result, Madrid's devastated industrial structure slowly started to come back to life.

With Franco, who was known as the Caudillo (Leader), ensconced in El Pardo – the stately home on the city's northwestern suburbs, which today serves as a museum of the Franco dictatorship as well as the official residence for visiting heads of state – Madrid went into a cultural nosedive. In the forty or so years prior to the outbreak of war in 1936, Madrid had been abuzz with literary and artistic excellence. The poet Federico García Lorca, film-maker Luis Buñuel, novelists Pío Baroja and Miguel de Unamuno, and the painters Pablo Picasso and Salvador Dalí had all achieved greatness during their years in Madrid. Before the civil war, many of them had lived and worked in the Residencia de Estudiantes, a haven for Madrid's avant-garde movement. The Residencia, located in what was then the northernmost reaches of the Paseo de Castellana, now the neighbourhood of Rationalist-style chalets known as El Viso, lives on as a hub for cultural activities in Madrid. In its day the Residencia gained wide international recognition, and it attracted distinguished visitors and lecturers such as Albert Einstein, Paul Valéry, Marie Curie, Igor Stravinsky, John Maynard Keynes and Le Corbusier.

Madrileños who mourned the city's paucity of culture – the fortunate ones who had survived the war and those who had not joined the exodus of intellectuals into exile – abruptly found their voices of dissent suffocated by the merriment of Madrid's new consumer society. The closing years of the 1950s saw the benefits of the Opus Dei technocrat government's *apertura*, the opening of the country's markets and beaches to the buoyant economies of postwar Europe and the U.S. One of the most momentous events was the launch in 1957 of the SEAT 600, a diminutive four-seater car made in Spain under licence by Fiat. The *Seiscientos*, as it was universally known, was the quintessential symbol of the Spanish 'economic miracle' that got underway in 1959, and which in less than fifteen years had sent Spain's annual GDP growth soaring to pole position among European countries. Before long Madrid's streets were choked with honking, fist-waving but proud owners of this badge on wheels of prosperity.

Property developers, never loath to slip envelopes under the table to Franco's corrupt planning officials, were quick to jump on the frenzy to reject a past that invoked memories of hunger and poverty. Throughout its history, the Paseo de la Castellana has gone through several name changes. With the Popular Front victory in 1936, it became known as Avenida de la Unión Proletaria. When Franco came to power in 1939 the name was changed to Avenida del Generalísimo. It was not until 1980 that the first democratically elected government after the dictator's death restored its original name. The Paseo del Prado and Paseo la Castellana, however, had always been the abode of Madrid's nobility, whose stately homes and gardens lined the avenues for 3.2 kilometres (2 mi.), from where the Palace Hotel now stands north to Paseo del General Martínez

Statue of the poet Federico García Lorca, in the Plaza de Santa Ana.

Campos. The wrecking ball came into action with vigour from the late 1940s to the early 1970s, reducing many architectural jewels to piles of rubble, in order to put up glass and steel office blocks and government buildings. The upshot is that 80 per cent of these small palaces have vanished. The nineteenth-century Palacio de Xifré, facing the Prado Museum, was one of Madrid's finest examples of the popular Moorish-revival style architecture Neo-Mudéjar. In 1949 it was purchased by a real estate firm that demolished it a year later to erect in its place the drab red-brick National Trade Union Office, now the Ministry of Health. The Palacio del Duque de Anglada, with its classic Grecian facade and Arab-style gardens modelled on the Patio de los Leones in the Alhambra, in the mid-1960s made way for the luxury Hotel Villa Magna.

American-style 'luncheonettes', erroneously labelled *cafeterías* (they were not, in fact, self-service), made their appearance in main shopping streets. Some bore the names of u.s. states: Cafetería California in Calle de Goya, Cafetería Nebraska in Calle de Bravo Murillo and so on. The 'quick bite to eat' culture had arrived. Office workers were forsaking their leisurely two-hour lunches, often taken at home, in favour of the *menú del día*, a fixed-price meal displayed on blackboards outside restaurants. By the 1970s, with the emergence of new commuter neighbourhoods, the afternoon siesta, too, had joined the ranks of vanishing species. Madrileños embraced their new-found affluence with a vengeance, enjoying a level of luxury they had not experienced since the pre-Civil War days.

These years were the best of times for Madrid's middle classes, albeit less so for blue-collar workers and university students. In the 1960s these groups began to take to the streets in protest against the dictatorship. The bourgeoisie was lulled into a lethargic state by a regime that placed no obstacles in the path of those who simply wanted to partake in the good life. This was personified in the clientele of the English-style Café Embassy in Calle de Ayala. The tearoom was founded in 1931 by Irishwoman Margarita Kearny Taylor, but in 2017 cut its last cucumber sandwich, forced out of business by spiralling rents in the Barrio de Salamanca. During the Second World War, Café Embassy was the rendezvous of spies from

El Corte Inglés

Each shopping district in Madrid has a branch of the country's foremost, indeed only, department store chain: El Corte Inglés. How this business came to dominate the sector is a typically Spanish tale of close family ties in business and provincial immigrants making good in Madrid. El Corte Inglés translates as 'the English cut'; originally a small tailor's, it opened in 1890 near the Puerta del Sol, providing Savile Row style for Madrid gentlemen – hence the name. In 1934 the business was bought by Ramón Areces Rodríguez, from Asturias on Spain's northern coast, and his uncle, César Rodríguez González. Areces had acquired his retailing skills in Cuba, working with his uncle in Havana's 'Almacenes El Encanto' department store.

After uncle and nephew had run the business for six years, everything had changed about the tailor's shop except the name, as it diversified to include a wide selection of clothing and accessories for men, women and children. Surviving the austerity of the 1940s and '50s, the store continued to grow, moving to a five-storey establishment at Calle Preciados, 3, where it fully developed into a modern department store. In the 1960s the business expanded with stores in Barcelona, Seville and Bilbao. El Corte Inglés has introduced many innovations to the Spanish shopper, such as Spain's first gift voucher in 1955 and a store charge card in 1967, a revolutionary idea, allowing customers to take their purchases home and only pay for them a month later. This developed into a credit card, and by 1991 El Corte Inglés was the largest issuer of credit cards in Spain.

For most of its history, the family kept tight control of the business, establishing an independent company to manufacture clothes for the stores. In 1995 El Corte Inglés bought out its long-time rival and only serious competitor Galerías Preciados, consolidating its position as the leading department store business in Spain. El Corte Inglés now has 92 department stores in Spain and two in Portugal, with more than 92,000 employees and a turnover of more than €15 billion.

El Corte Inglés in Calle Preciados, 1950s.

Gran Vía in the 1960s.

the Nazi as well as Allied camps. From the post-war years until its closure, the café catered to local 'ladies who lunch' clad in fur, and cigar-smoking entrepreneurs in their ubiquitous dark-green loden coats. Afternoon tea and scones were served with jam and cream, for customers who had returned from a London holiday with newly acquired tastes.

It was the Franco regime's laissez-faire attitude to the middle classes that laid the groundwork for a smooth transition to democratic government. The new economic order meant that people could afford to take short holiday breaks in London, Paris or New York. Many returned in an angry and resentful mood, having ventured beyond the Pyrenees to places that enjoyed a free press, without grey-uniformed policemen in the streets clutching submachine guns, and where government opponents did not have to speak in whispers in cafés. They would quietly bide their time, knowing that the days of the ageing dictator, who was stricken with phlebitis and Parkinson's disease, were numbered.

7 We Go Movida Along

On a frosty December morning in 1973, Admiral Luis Carrero Blanco left Madrid's San Francisco de Borja Church in Calle de Serrano, where he attended daily Mass, to be driven just over a kilometre to government headquarters at the Palacio de Villamejor in Paseo de la Castellana. Six months previously Franco had appointed his trusty colleague prime minister, with the expectation that the admiral would eventually succeed the eighty-year-old Caudillo, who was in failing health.

Carrero Blanco had breached a fundamental security rule by following the same route every day from the church to his office. As the Dodge 3700 saloon turned into Calle de Claudio Coello, in the heart of the Barrio de Salamanca, three guerrillas from the Basque separatist movement ETA crouched in a basement flat watching in horror as a mother pushed a pram along the street. Fortunately, the woman soon reached the corner, and was well out of range when Carrero Blanco's car passed over the spot where the militants had placed 90 kilograms (200 lb) of high explosives in a tunnel under the road that they had spent five months digging. The blast sent the car flying 30 metres (100 ft) into the air, where it briefly came to rest on the rooftop of a Jesuit hall of residence before tumbling into the courtyard. The powerful bomb left a crater in the road 8 metres (26 ft) deep and killed Carrero Blanco's driver and bodyguard. The primary target survived the attack, but only for a few minutes. By the time the police arrived on the scene, he had died of his injuries. ETA had delivered a lethal blow to the Franco regime, for Carrero Blanco, nicknamed the 'Ogre' by his enemies, was an unreconstructed hardliner. Had he lived to take the helm after the Generalísimo's death two years later, Spain would have faced a much rockier road back to democracy.

At last, in the autumn of 1975, the long-awaited moment had arrived. Franco lay dying in Madrid's Hospital La Paz, at the top of Paseo de la Castellana. It took the dictator the better part of a month in his hospital bed to shuffle off this mortal coil. At one point, before slipping into a coma from which he never emerged, he was reported to have moaned to his surgeons, 'My God, how difficult this is!' Finally, shortly after midnight on 20 November 1975, the dictator's family agreed to have his life support disconnected.

A tense calm descended on Madrid in the days following the announcement of Franco's demise. Journalists who would habitually gather after work at the Café Roma, across the road from the EFE state news agency in Calle de Ayala, exchanged banter in hushed voices, for fear of being overheard by members of right-wing groups or government informers – in the early Franco days, the café was a

Devastation after the assassination of Prime Minister Luis Carrero Blanco, 20 December 1973.

rendezvous for Falangist intellectuals like the writers José María Pemán and Rafael Sánchez Mazas. Following the Caudillo's death in 1975, Francoist thugs from the Guerrilleros de Cristo Rey (Warriors of Christ the King), Fuerza Nueva (New Force) and other extremist bands roamed the streets, on the lookout for any manifestation of anti-regime activity. It was not long before the worst of these fears were borne out. On a January night in 1977, more than a year later, nine labour lawyers belonging to the Comisiones Obreras (Workers' Commissions) Communist trade union were finishing up a meeting in their office in Calle de Atocha, near the Plaza Mayor. Without warning, three masked men armed with sub-machine guns burst into the office and shot dead five of the lawyers, leaving the other four critically wounded. The massacre brought hundreds of thousands of Madrileños into the streets in a protest march. In 1978 the events were adapted for cinema by Juan Antonio Bardem in his film *Siete días de enero* (Seven Days in January). A monument to the victims was later erected in Calle de Atocha outside the Antón Martín Metro station. It spoke hopefully of Spain's fledgling democracy that the gunmen were rounded up and sentenced to a total of 464 years in prison. This was the first time pro-Franco extremists had been put on trial since the dictator's death.

Madrid was to know even more extreme backlashes from Franco diehards in the coming years, culminating in a farcical, Buster Keaton-style coup attempt by elements within the armed forces in 1981. For now, at least, Madrileños were determined to make up for the low cultural ebb in which the city had drifted for decades. Press censorship remained in force throughout the final years of the dictatorship. The most disgraceful incident was the closure of the newspaper *Madrid*. The city's only evening daily took a subtle, read-between-the-lines policy on Franco and his regime. In 1971 its reformist-minded proprietor, the philosophy professor Rafael Calvo Serer, published an editorial suggesting France's ageing and increasingly unpopular leader Charles de Gaulle should resign. The paper took the bold step of asserting that the situation in France bore marked similarities to that of Franco's Spain. *Madrid* was summarily forced to shut and its headquarters in the Barrio de Salamanca was sold to a property developer and demolished to make way for a block of luxury flats.

Even before Franco's death, the cinema had overtaken Madrid's addiction to the theatre as the most popular medium of entertainment outside the home. Until 1977, however, the film industry was encumbered by strict government censorship. Dubbing was mandatory for foreign-language films, a practice employed to control any dialogue that might expose an audience to subversive ideas. Even today in Spanish cinemas, dubbing is more the rule than the exception. The industry is firmly in the grip of a band of highly paid professionals, lambasted as a 'mafia' by advocates of subtitled films.

So-called 'v.o.' (original version) cinemas showing subtitled films began popping up around Madrid in the 1980s. They were mostly fitted with plush interiors for pre-show drinks and chit-chat, as a rendezvous point for relaxed socializing as well as movie-going. The most notable ones are the multiscreen Cines Verdi in Calle de Bravo Murillo, Cine Ideal in Calle del Doctor Cortezo and three Cine Renoir cinemas specializing in avant-garde film. Without a shadow of a doubt, the most spectacular addition to the Madrid cinema scene is Cine Doré, whose ochre and cream Art Nouveau facade is a wonder to behold. This was Madrid's first cinema, which got its start in the late nineteenth century under licence to the French film-makers the Lumière brothers. The original auditorium was located in the basement of the long-vanished Hotel Rusia in the Carrera de San Jerónimo. The cinema moved its premises to Calle de Santa Isabel, its present location, in 1912. Most of the regular patrons were local residents of the working-class Embajadores district. The cinema acquired the derogatory nickname *Palacio de las pipas* (Pumpkin Seed Palace), so-called for the piles of pumpkin seed shells deposited on the carpeted floor after each film showing, in the days when Madrileños were obsessed with munching these seeds. After a closure of nearly twenty years, the Doré was given a refit in the early 1980s and reopened in 1989 as the classiest of Madrid cinemas.

In the late 1970s something was bubbling in Madrid, the likes of which the city had not known since the pre-war days of the Republic. The release of pent-up energy after decades of Franco-weariness

Monument to the labour lawyers murdered by right-wing terrorists in 1977.

came about like a force of nature. Its name was *La Movida*. The slang word is an invention of the early 1980s – it does not appear in the dictionary of the Royal Academy. The closest English equivalent would be 'the scene', or perhaps 'the movement', taken in a cultural and not a political sense. Two events that took place in Madrid in 1980 gave both definitions to this movement. A memorial concert for the Madrid rock composer and drummer of the band Tos, José

Cine Doré, Calle de Santa Isabel.

Luis Cano Leal, known as *Canito*, brought together for the first time some of the artists and groups that came to symbolize *La Movida*: Nacha Pop, Alaska y los Pegamoides, Mermelada, Paraíso and Los Bólidos. The British journalist and author John Hooper noted, 'The most obvious sign of a new mood was to be found in the phenomenon known as the *movida madrileña* [a punk-rock counterculture sound that recalled the British New Wave of the late 1970s].'

The year 1980 also saw the release of Pedro Almodóvar's first feature film, *Pepi, Luci, Bom y otras chicas del montón* (Pepi, Luci, Bom and Other Girls in the Gang). It starred Carmen Maura, Cecilia Roth, Alaska and others who featured in his future films and came to be known collectively as 'Almodóvar's girls'. This high-camp and somewhat dark comedy, set in Madrid, was destined to become an

Cine Ideal, Calle
del Doctor Cortezo.

inspiration for a decade of hedonistic partying. Almodóvar, more
than any other artist of the day, embodied the capital's spirit of 'anything goes' liberation. The streets of Malasaña and Chueca echoed
with battle cries of *Madrid nunca duerme* (Madrid never sleeps),
Esta noche todo el mundo a la calle (Tonight, everybody into the
streets) and *Madrid me mata* (Madrid is killing me), which was also
the title of a magazine. The somewhat pretentious notion of Madrid
as the cultural capital of the world was widespread in *La Movida*,
which in a way resembled a throwback to the counterculture movement of the 1960s and the 'Cool Britannia' that emerged in British
cities in the 1990s. Recreational drugs, social protest, homosexuality
in public – anything that was taboo under Franco's regime was taken
up with a passion by Madrid's youth.

Lieutenant Colonel Antonio Tejero in the Chamber of Deputies, 23 February 1981.

Street artists flourished during *La Movida*. There was no longer the fear of being attacked by the police, a possibility that had weighed heavy on graffitists since 1976, when a young man was shot dead when caught painting an anti-Franco slogan on a wall. The most celebrated graffiti artist was known as *Muelle*, as revered in Madrid as Banksy has been in later years. He was famous for his signature, which years after his death in 1995 enjoys an unofficial protected status and whose pale outlines can still be observed on a few walls across the city.

Then, on the night of 23 February 1981, the merry-making came to a screeching halt. It was almost inevitable that the wave of unbridled rejoicing and licentiousness that had swept Madrid and the rest of Spain would sooner or later incite a backlash from entrenched Franco-regime loyalists, branded by the media as *El Búnker*. While Madrid youth partied in the clubs of Malasaña, dark forces in the military and the intransigent far right were conspiring to put an end to what they reviled as degenerate and immoral revelling.

Parliament had been called into session that February evening to vote on the investiture of centre-right politician Leopoldo Calvo-Sotelo as prime minister. He had been chosen to replace Adolfo Suárez, Spain's first democratically elected leader since the Second Republic, who had resigned after five years in office. Without warning, at 6:30 p.m. a detachment of civil guardsmen led by Lieutenant Colonel Antonio Tejero burst into the Chamber of Deputies, brandishing sub-machine guns. Tejero, looking a caricature of himself with his three-cornered patent leather hat and bushy moustache, shouted, 'Everyone down on the floor!' All but three deputies swiftly ducked under their seats. The exceptions were Spanish Communist Party (PCE) Secretary-General Santiago Carrillo, who later explained that he had nothing to lose, for if the coup had succeeded he was a doomed man; Prime Minister Suárez, a former senior figure in the Franco government and chairman of the state-controlled television network, who had foreseen the need for democratic reform; and Deputy Prime Minister Lieutenant General Manuel Gutiérrez Mellado, who not only refused to obey the command but marched down to the podium to try to wrest Tejero's revolver from his hand. This triggered a burst of machine-gun fire by one of the civil guardsmen, leaving bullet holes in the ceiling that, to this day, have not been plastered over.

A cluster of journalists crowded the entrance of the Hotel Palace across the road from the Cortes, observing the ring of civil guardsmen posted around parliament. The green-uniformed paramilitary troops looked more bewildered than threatening, seemingly unsure whether to point their weapons at the Chamber of Deputies or the crowds of onlookers gathered outside the building. The unsung hero of that night was chief of police José Antonio Sáenz de Santamaría, whose men, armed with sub-machine guns, were sent in to throw a cordon around the civil guard, just in case they became trigger-happy. Three and a half hours after the storming of parliament, King Juan Carlos, in his field marshal uniform, went on television to condemn the attempted coup and order back to barracks those army units that had been deployed in the streets by a handful of insurgent generals. From that moment, the attempted coup was doomed to failure. Throughout the night, civil guardsmen could be seen clambering out of windows and dashing up the darkened streets behind the parliament building. Tejero himself held out until midday on 24 February, when he finally surrendered and was subsequently sentenced to thirty years in prison. So ended the last serious attempt by Franco loyalists to sabotage Spain's future as a democracy. Madrid now had good cause to celebrate. The following evening, tens of thousands of Madrileños gathered outside the Cortes to shout *¡vivas!* for democracy, after which many made off for the once again vibrant night spots of Malasaña and Chueca.

The centre of gravity of *La Movida* was in the city's nightspots, from which it took its name, particularly the now defunct Rock-Ola Club. A still-bouncing survivor is El Pentagrama in Malasaña's Calle de la Palma, whose 9 p.m. to 3:30 a.m. opening hours continue unchanged. This club, whose walls are decorated with photos of David Bowie and Blondie, was a hot spot of Madrid's frenetic night-life throughout the 1980s. Its early morning sessions always finished with Bill Haley's 'See You Later, Alligator'.

This was not a movement orchestrated by any single celebrity, avant-garde film producer or rock group. On the contrary, what gave rise to and fuelled *La Movida* was exactly the opposite, the lack of an oppressive government. There was, however, one person whose goodwill and spirited support kept the party rolling from 1979 to 1986, the years in which he presided over city hall as the most popular mayor in Madrid's history: Enrique Tierno Galván. Under the guidance and inspiration of this soft-spoken university professor, who fought for the Republic during the war, Madrid transformed itself into a leading world metropolis of culture and the arts. From the day this avuncular Socialist stepped into office until his death seven years later, the number of visitors to the Museo de Arte Contemporáneo (Contemporary Arts Museum) soared by 525 per cent, visits to the Prado Museum increased 61 per cent and even the Museo Arqueológico (Archaeological Museum) saw a 71 per cent jump in visitors. Madrileños flocked by their thousands to exhibitions at Madrid's more than 230 art galleries, exhibition halls and publicly funded institutions, like the Museo Municipal, Centro Cultural de la Villa (Madrid Cultural Centre), Conde Duque and the Círculo de Bellas Artes (Fine Arts Centre).

Tierno Galván, known affectionately to Madrileños as *El Viejo Profesor* (The Old Professor) took Madrid's cultural offering to a level at which, in his own words, 'one can pass the entire day without spending a penny, going from exhibition to exhibition, viewing sculptures, paintings and other arts, as well as historical displays'. In the Mayor's esteem, Madrid had become 'one of the most prestigious cities in Europe'. The Tierno Galván years also brought a revival of Madrid's festivals, such as the reinstatement of the carnival and a dozen or so others that were discouraged, if not banned outright, by the dictatorship. This included the city's first Festival of Erotica in 1985, held in what is now the Fernán Gómez Cultural Centre in Plaza de Colón, at which Tierno Galván offered a word of welcome – before making a discreet exit.

The mayor dug deep into the city's coffers to finance badly needed urban redevelopment. As early as 1982, he had authorized home-refurbishment subsidies of up to 20 per cent to residents of the Barrio de las Letras, Chueca, Malasaña and other inner-city neighbourhoods. This was a first, not only for Madrid but for Spain as a whole, a country that traditionally allows historic buildings to fall into disrepair and be demolished by property speculators. A good part of these classic barrios of Madrid have been done up to a standard that inspires their residents' pride, and they have become home to an eclectic mix of traditional lower-middle-class families, arty and media types and young professionals. The once dilapidated streets around Calle de Segovia and Plaza de la Paja, for instance, shine as an example of architectural recovery and civic self-esteem. In 1985 the unsightly fly-over at the Atocha railway station, which had always served as a shadowy haven for muggers and beggars, was dismantled. The area around Atocha almost overnight became a highly desirable neighbourhood, with property prices to match. More than 6,000 new dwellings were constructed for low-income families in the southern districts of Villaverde, Orcasitas and Vallecas,

The mayor of Madrid, Enrique Tierno Galván, in Plaza de la Villa.

Enrique Tierno Galván

Enrique Tierno Galván's gentle and self-effacing charisma won the hearts of Madrileños during the seven years he served as the city's mayor. His mandate, from 1979 to 1986, coincided with the most difficult time of Spain's transition from a fossilized military dictatorship to a modern European democracy. He bore no grudges, despite having been expelled from his post at the University of Madrid in 1965 after voicing support for anti-government student protests. He took up a lectureship at Princeton University and returned to Spain in 1968, with Franco still in power, to secretly found the Popular Socialist Party (PSP). Tierno Galván's *bandos*, or municipal pronouncements, written in a florid, archaic style, endeared the mayor to his constituency. They represented a refreshing and effective tool for communicating with a people accustomed to threats and bullying from officialdom. The *bandos* were issued by 'The Mayor of the Most Excellent City Hall of Madrid' and always began with '¡Madrileños!' His first, dealing with the problem of litter, exhorted the citizenry 'to comply with what a proper upbringing and civic education require, and to remind those lacking in these virtues of their responsibilities.' One of the mayor's last *bandos* invited the people of Madrid to celebrate their brotherhood with Europe: 'Your mayor beseeches and supplicates you to display your joy and give testimony that we are part of Europe and adhere to the destiny of so many and so noble a people.' Tierno Galván's lively sense of humour was always in evidence, even on his deathbed. In his final days in hospital, a journalist asked him whether as an atheist, he feared death. 'Not at all,' he replied, 'for I know God has a soft spot for atheists.'

while the Metro was extended to inner suburbs that previously had only been served by public buses.

Tierno Galván was arguably Madrid's greatest benefactor since King Carlos III. It speaks volumes of his popularity that more than a million Madrileños turned out for his funeral in January 1986. His gravestone bears the simple inscription he had requested: Enrique Tierno Galván, *Alcalde de Madrid* (Mayor of Madrid). The Old Professor's statue stands in a park named after him. It was appropriately built near the Railway Museum in Legazpi, one of the poorer districts of the city's southern sector that had benefited from his investment programmes.

By the early 1990s *La Movida* had gone the way of all fads. The death of Tierno Galván deprived its followers of a dynamo who sanctioned and stimulated the movement. *La Movida* went on the wane, to give way to other priorities. The media was now focused on Spain's role in Europe, particularly on the challenge of gaining membership to the EC (the European Community, predecessor of the European Union) and NATO – goals which were both achieved under the Socialist government of Felipe González. The 1981 failed coup had served as a wake-up call, reminding people that work was still needed to bring Spain into the mainstream of European democracies.

8 Madrid Gets a Facelift

Tierno Galván had set in motion a series of actions aimed at improving the lot of Madrid's less affluent citizens. But the Old Professor's tenure in office was too short-lived to achieve all the goals set out in his ambitious blueprint. His 1985 General Town Planning project oversaw the construction of nearly 13,000 new dwellings in the poorer areas south of the city centre. The Special Plan for the Protection and Preservation of Historic Buildings put the brakes on the unrestrained demolition jamboree of the Franco years. The Atocha fly-over eyesore was dismantled and a tunnel was built between Ronda de Valencia and Paseo de María Cristina, to ease traffic congestion in one of the busiest approaches to central Madrid. Still, much remained to be done to make Madrid a more habitable place to live.

The early 1990s marked the take-off of urban regeneration projects, in tandem with a cultural boom the likes of which the city had never known. The mayoral elections of 1991 brought a 180-degree shift in municipal politics, with the absolute majority win by the right-wing Popular Party candidate José María Álvarez del Manzano. He came to office after several rather bland predecessors had failed to win the hearts of Madrileños, and thanks to the demise of the centrist Centro Democrático y Social (CDS), whose supporters gave their vote to Manzano as the 'lesser of two evils' against the Socialist and radical left candidates. Manzano was in office from 1991 to 2003, making him the longest-serving mayor in Madrid's history to date. The 1990s saw the construction of the 32-kilometre (20-mi.) M-30 ring road, the busiest in Spain. In the following decade, major upgrade works

Sol Metro sign.

took place, giving the M-30 Europe's longest motorway tunnels, with sections almost 6 kilometres (4 mi.) in length with three to six lanes in each direction. The M-30 was later encircled by the M-40 and M-50 outer ring roads.

There was a time, not so many years ago, when a journey on the Madrid Metro was a dismal undertaking, something best avoided unless it was absolutely necessary. The underground transport system was used mostly by those who lacked an alternative means of transport for their daily journey to and from the city centre. It was said that the Metro offered only one reliable feature: trains would always enter the station from the right. While Madrid's motorists switched from driving on the left to the right in 1924, the Metro lines carried on operating on the left-hand side, as they do today. The Metro had been a victim of neglect by civic authorities since the 1960s, when the arrival of the SEAT 600 had sparked a frenzy of car ownership. There is still in some circles a lingering sense of loss of status attached to using the Metro, albeit this is confined to a tiny segment of the population. For instance, it would be a rare sight indeed to spot a senior bank executive commuting to work in this way.

At the beginning of the 1990s control of the network was transferred to a public enterprise, Metro de Madrid, through which large-scale expansion projects were carried out. This became the driving force behind the Metro's expansion from the 1990s onward, which has since endowed the city with 290 kilometres (180 mi.) of track, 301 stations and thirteen lines, with more than 2,300 trains carrying around 2 million passengers a day. In the early 2000s a huge project installed approximately 50 kilometres (31 mi.) of new Metro tunnels. Crucially, this work included a direct link between Madrid and the airport from Nuevos Ministerios Metro station, as well as connections from other lines. It also increased services to the outskirts, with a huge 40-kilometre (25-mi.) loop called MetroSur serving Madrid's southern suburbs. MetroSur, one of the largest ever civil engineering projects in Europe, opened in 2003. It is comprised of 28 new stations, including an interchange station that connects the city centre to the local commuter rail network. The expanded network also provides services to Getafe, Móstoles, Alcorcón, Fuenlabrada and Leganés, five outer suburbs south of Madrid.

Likewise on the transportation front, the 1990s saw the transformation of Madrid Barajas Adolfo Suárez airport into a major cargo hub, with the construction of its first freight terminal alongside a new control tower and a fourth runway. But these initiatives paled into insignificance compared with the great infrastructural event of 2006, when Terminal 4 entered into service. This was a vast undertaking designed by the British architect Richard Rogers and his Spanish colleagues Antonio Lamela and Luis Vidal, who won Britain's Stirling Prize for excellence in architecture. Terminal 4 looks the size of a small country, one of the world's largest airport terminals, with 752,500 square metres (8.1 million sq. ft) in separate landside and airside structures.

Two landmark events in railway infrastructure improvement took place in 1992, the year Madrid held the title of European Capital of Culture. The first was the opening of the new Atocha railway station following the complete overhaul of the 140-year-old building. The station, whose name comes from the nearby Church of

Our Lady of Atocha, had stood in a sorry state of disrepair until the international award-winning architect Rafael Moneo, who later designed the Prado Museum expansion of 2007, was commissioned to create a new terminal. The original building was converted into a shopping concourse with boutiques and cafés and decorated with a sumptuous 4,000-square-metre (43,000-sq.-ft) covered tropical garden. Moneo also designed the terminal built on adjacent land to serve the new AVE trains and local commuter lines. AVE stands for *Alta Velocidad Española* (Spanish High Speed), and is a play on the Spanish word *ave*, meaning 'bird'. The first AVE was put into service in 1992, linking Madrid to Seville at speeds of up to 310 kilometres per hour (193 mph). Madrid has now become the terminus for Spain's high-speed rail service. With 3,240 kilometres (2,013 mi.) of operational track, and a further 2,285 kilometres (1,420 mi.) under construction, it ranks as the most extensive in Europe and second only worldwide to China's over 29,000-kilometre (9,942-mi.) high-speed rail network.

The expansion and upgrading of the Metro and commuter rail services meant that by the mid-1990s Madrileños could enjoy one of Europe's most efficient and low-cost public transport systems. No longer would people have to battle the massive traffic snarls that blocked the road approaches to the city, nor pay exorbitant fees in underground car parks. Yet people were disinclined to give up their cars and, in some cases, they would go to extraordinary lengths to inflict on themselves a tiresome and costly journey to the office.

The picaresque novel originated in Madrid in the seventeenth century. Francisco de Quevedo and Miguel de Cervantes were the two celebrated precursors of this genre, which featured as its hero a rogue who employs every imaginable bit of trickery to achieve his purposes. It would appear that the picaresque gene remains embedded in the DNA of many Madrileños. In 1994 a new lane was opened on the N-VI motorway that connects the northern commuter belt to the city. The lane is restricted to peak-hour traffic and for cars with two or more occupants. Before long, stories began to appear in the

Interior tropical gardens of Atocha Railway Station.

Atocha station memorial.

press of the civil guard pulling over cars with suspicious-looking passengers, who turned out to be mannequins.

The Atocha revamp and expansion was one of Madrid's proudest achievements of its transport modernization programme. No one could suspect what lay in store for it on the morning of 11 March 2004, when the station was struck a violent blow. During the peak rush hour, four commuter trains entering Atocha were blown to pieces by ten bombs. The government, which was facing a general election in three days' time, immediately pinned the blame on Basque separatist guerrillas. The accusation was unconvincing: the 1973 bomb that killed Admiral Carrero Blanco had, in a perverse way, made a kind of sense. After all, he was the symbol of the Franco regime's continuity, hence a logical ETA target. In the ensuing years numerous police and civil guards fell victim to the Basque guerrillas, all of them branded as 'enemies of *Euskalherria*' (Basque Homeland). But these were commuter trains, packed with ordinary blue- and white-collar workers, many of them Eastern European and Latin American immigrants. This was not ETA's style and the Basque terrorists promptly denied all responsibility for the attacks. The ruling conservative Popular Party (PP) was anxious to quash speculation about Islamist involvement, fearing it would be seen as a consequence of their having taken Spain into the Iraq war a year previously. When it emerged that the bombings had indeed been carried out by Islamist terrorists, the PP were swept from office by the Socialists.

On the night of the attack, tens of thousands of Madrileños marched to Atocha, where they held a silent vigil. No calls for revenge were heard from the crowds, there were no outcries of anger: instead, the prevailing mood was one of sombre dignity. Then, Madrid being Madrid, when the last candles were extinguished and people hunched up against the cold rain that lashed the vast station piazza, the crowds dispersed under their umbrellas to the many bars and restaurants of the Atocha district. An 11-metre (36-ft) memorial to the victims of the attack was erected at the station, an illuminated cylinder engraved with hundreds of messages of sympathy. The shrine has won praise for its innovative design and pioneering use of materials, including the fluorine-based ethylene tetrafluoroethylene (ETFE) used in the membrane.

Madrid becoming the first Spanish city to be voted European Capital of Culture was cause for great celebration. Some held to the belief that it was *La Movida*'s international reverberations that had thrust Madrid to centre stage in Europe. Others argued, perhaps more convincingly, that the award was given in recognition of the city's great cultural triumphs of the new decade. The year 1992 saw the completion of the 'Golden Triangle', the name given to the three world-class museums to be found within a ten-minute walk of one another along or next to the Paseo del Prado. The superstar is, of course, the Prado Museum, whose magnificence is now complemented and amplified by the arrival of the two other vertices of the triangle.

The Museo Nacional Centro de Arte Reina Sofía, found near the Atocha railway station, was inaugurated by King Juan Carlos and

Crowd outside the Reina Sofía Museum.

Queen Sofía, the museum bearing the queen's name. The building itself had been erected in the eighteenth century as the Hospital de San Carlos and was designed by architects José de Hermosilla and Francesco Sabatini in characteristically sombre Neoclassical style. It served as a hospital until 1965, and for more than a decade afterwards the threat of demolition hung over it, until in 1977 the government declared it a national monument. Prior to its official opening in 1992, the current Reina Sofía functioned as a centre for contemporary art exhibitions. The Reina Sofía was an instant success from its inauguration, so much so that in 2001 the French architect Jean Nouvel was brought in to design a new building that expanded the museum's exhibition space by more than 60 per cent. The top visitor attraction of the museum's collection of more than 21,700 works is Pablo Picasso's monumental *Guernica*, painted in 1937. The mural-sized 349 × 777-centimetre (137 × 306-in.) canvas depicts the horrors of the bombing of the Basque town of Guernica at the height of the Spanish Civil War.

In that stellar year of 1992 the Thyssen-Bornemisza Museum also opened its doors, almost directly across the road from the Prado Museum. The gallery, located in the headquarters of a failed bank, is named after its founder, the German-Hungarian entrepreneur Baron Thyssen Bornemisza (1921–2002). The institution began its life with a comparatively modest display of some seven hundred works of art, many of which were brought to Madrid from the family collection. The Baron's wife, the former 'Miss Spain' winner Carmen Cervera, later gave on loan more than four hundred works from her private collection to the museum. The original paintings on display included works by some of Europe's most prestigious Old Masters, including Michelangelo, Caravaggio, Dürer and Van Dyck. The museum has since expanded to include more modern pieces, including many Impressionist masterpieces, to bring the total collection to more than a thousand works of art. The Reina Sofía, featuring twentieth-century art, and the Thyssen-Bornemisza, with some of the best Impressionist, Expressionist, European and American paintings from the second half of the last century, complement the Prado's collection of pre-twentieth-century Old Masters.

The city is an eminently walkable place. In less than half an hour, a stroll across the Retiro Park near the Barrio de Salamanca leads to any of the best-known cafés, restaurants and shopping streets. The expanse beyond the Plaza de Castilla to the north, or eastward on the road to the airport, was uncharted territory, a virtually uninhabited wasteland as late as the 1960s, when the area between the Nuevos Ministerios and Plaza de Castilla was nothing but a vast Gypsy encampment. It therefore came as no small surprise on a journey into town from the airport in 1998 to discover a Metro station called Campo de las Naciones, now changed to Feria de Madrid. This was one of the municipal planners' early efforts to decentralize Madrid's business and leisure activities. The authorities had decided to take a hand in enhancing Madrid's appeal as a business centre, but away from the inner city's congested neighbourhoods.

The Feria de Madrid area, a five-minute Metro journey from the airport, gave Madrid a new and badly needed conference centre, the Palacio Municipal de Congresos. Since its inauguration in 1993 the centre has hosted conferences of the IMF, the World Bank, the EU, NATO and the United Nations. New recreational facilities were added in the vicinity of the conference centre. The old Olivar de la

Hinojosa golf course was transformed into the 220-hectare (544-ac.) King Juan Carlos I Park, with two lakes, a small river, smart gardens, cybernetic fountains and an events hall with a 23,000 seating capacity. In 2006 the promoters changed the name of the complex to Madrid Espacios y Congresos (Madrid Spaces and Conferences), to reinforce its identity as a key component of Madrid's business tourism sector, placing the emphasis on a wider range of activities. The idea was to boost Madrid's international profile in the events sector, from international tennis tournaments to gastronomy fairs.

Hard on the heels of the recovery of the airport area, Britain's Norman Foster and the American Henry N. Cobb, along with a team of eminent Spanish architects, were commissioned to design a cluster of commercial skyscrapers called the Cuatro Torres (Four Towers). When the project was completed in 2008 (a fifth tower was opened in 2019), it added 300,00 square metres (3.2 million sq. ft) of office space onto what was once the training ground of the Real Madrid football team. The new building relieved pressure on central Madrid's congested business district, above all in and around the Paseo de la Castellana. The towers quickly attracted big-name multinationals, including British American Tobacco, PricewaterhouseCoopers, MasterCard, Commerzbank and Coca-Cola. The Four Towers are the first feature a visitor will see when coming in to land at Madrid airport or from the northern motorway approach to the city. Mercifully, this gargantuan imitation of London's Canary Wharf and Paris's La Défense is hidden from view from mostly anywhere in the city centre.

In the late sixteenth century, Madrid was a city of shopkeepers – stallholders, to be precise. The Plaza del Arrabal, now the Plaza Mayor, is where locals went to have their boots mended, purchase fabric to fashion their clothes or acquire earthenware kitchen pots and the like. Madrid's royal treasury was also the depository for the silver and gold shipped to Spain from its colonies. Heavy industry, such as shipbuilding and the manufacture of armour and weapons, was virtually unknown in the capital. The city's economic profile changed little over the following centuries, until the extreme centralization of the Franco years began to attract manufacturing industries

The Four Towers with a wall of graffiti below.

to Madrid. In order to obtain a factory permit, official subsidies or political favours, you needed to be close to the seat of power.

By the late 1990s little was left of the industrial Madrid that had been built up over the preceding decades. Almost all major multi-nationals operating in Spain have their headquarters in the capital, but their assembly plants and factories have moved out of the city, to take advantage of lower land costs and in some cases, proximity to sea ports. Madrid is now one of Europe's most intensely service-centred capital cities. All that is left in the southern districts of Legazpi, Carabanchel and Vallecas are a handful of cottage indus-tries. By 2002 Madrid was the largest contributor to GDP of all Spain's seventeen semi-autonomous regions. The city has become the country's economic heartland, a phenomenon that came about with the return to its roots. The financial powerhouse of the days of empire is now home to the leading Spanish and international banks and investment funds.

Moving into the twenty-first century, one of the most impressive undertakings rolled out by city planners was the reinvention of the Palacio de Comunicaciones, more commonly known as Correos y Telégrafos (Postal and Telegraphic Services), which was its function until 2003 when it was renamed Palacio de Cibeles. Until then, visitors to the Plaza de Cibeles could be seen staring in disbelief when it was pointed out that this bombastic architectural gem of the Belle Epoque was the city's central post office. The 30,000-square-metre (323,000-sq.-ft) complex, with a richly ornamented Neo-Plateresque facade and Baroque towers, was one of the first buildings of its style to be erected in the city centre. It represents the vitality and imagination that continue to drive Madrid forward in the face of political and economic vicissitudes.

Madrid's City Hall shifted its headquarters in 2007 from Plaza de la Villa to the refurbished Palacio de Cibeles, where the mayor's office now occupies one wing of the building. At the same time, the central post office moved to Feria de Madrid and a Postal and Telegraph Museum was opened in Aravaca, a district some 10 kilometres (6 mi.) west of the city centre. The highlight of the redesigned Palacio, which was completed in 2011, is a cultural space, open to the public, called CentroCentro. This is an outstanding example of how a building from the beginning of the twentieth century can be brought up to date with contemporary, sustainable building strategies, from green materials and natural-light optimization to resource conservation and energy-efficient systems.

The Palacio de Cibeles complements the 'Golden Triangle' of art museums. The building retains many of its original features, together with new additions, most notably the striking 930-square-metre (10,000-sq.-ft) crystal gallery roof above the building's rear section. The front and rear facing the central courtyard have been fitted out as leisure centres, where visitors can go to learn about the cultural activities the city has to offer. This visitor-friendly area offers a workplace with sofas and armchairs, worktables, newspapers,

Rooftop bar and lounge at Palacio de Cibeles.

magazines and a café. Visitors can climb the 70-metre (230-ft) spiral staircase of the central tower, up to a terraced area that offers a splendid view over the city, at its most dramatic on one of Madrid's many clear, starlit nights.

The Palacio de Cibeles ranks high as one of the true glories of Madrid – high also in the sense that its outdoor bar is one of the city's loftiest, offering an unmatched panoramic view of Calle de Alcalá, Gran Vía and Paseo de la Castellana. From sunset to the wee hours, here you will find Madrileños sprawled on chaises longues, indulging their passion for gin and tonic, which in Madrid has been raised to an art form. Depending on which direction you look, the rooftop terraces that have blossomed in recent times are abundantly in evidence. You may see an identical scene taking place on top of the Círculo de Bellas Artes in Calle de Alcalá, or the Hotel H10 Puerta de Alcalá up the same street, or the terrace of the Hotel Reina Victoria in Plaza de Santa Ana, or even a faint glimmer of merriment from numerous other terraces in the hip neighbourhoods of Chueca and Malasaña. This ritual has never flagged – even in the worst years of the recession Madrid suffered from 2008 to 2014. It would take more than a global financial meltdown to deter a Madrileño from a night on the town. In those dark days booking was always a must at any top-rated restaurant in the city centre. You would feel lonely and neglected indeed if you turned up at nine o'clock for dinner, the first in the restaurant.

How do they do it? For more than thirty years, since Spain's accession to the EEC in 1986, Madrileños have been putting in regular European working hours. The afternoon siesta became a thing of the past well before that time. How is it that the worst traffic jams in the city's liveliest neighbourhoods begin building up after midnight? How do people get by without sleeping? The surprising fact is that, despite the late-night culture, Madrid is on a par with the European average level of productivity. A persuasive explanation has to do with psychological conflict. People in Berlin and London, to cite two examples, put an enormous amount of time and energy into earning a living. In scant moments of reflection, they realize that this lifestyle is flawed and that the enjoyment derived from their daily routine is not commensurate with the sweat and toil put into simply staying ahead. The only time they have to work out this dilemma is at night, hence the need for a proper night's sleep. Madrileños, it would appear, are not troubled by these conflicts. Their credo, in the spirit of John Dryden's poem, 'Happy The Man' (1685), would be: 'Tomorrow, do thy worst, for I have lived today.'

THE CITY TODAY

Aerial view of Plaza Mayor and surrounding rooftops.

Squares

The term 'square' is a misnomer when talking about Madrid's traditional hubs of social interaction. Few, if any, fit this profile. Hence the Spanish word *plaza*, which can be translated as 'open space', would be a more accurate description.

Among the city's most iconic landmarks, the Plaza Mayor comes closest to what might be called a true 'square'. But in fact, it is an enormous rectangle, which got its start as the first public space built inside the walls erected by the Moors. This was a spot for social gatherings, often of a macabre nature. Families would come on Sundays to watch public executions by garrotting or hanging and, on special occasions, they would be treated to a heretic burning. The plaza later served as a bullring, a spectacle that could be viewed from the 237 balconies that surround the square.

Today, the Plaza Mayor is a setting for the far more serene spectator sport of people-watching. Its many cafés make an ideal viewpoint for observing buskers, acrobats, groups of youths and not-so-young people dashing off to the bars along the adjacent Calle de Cuchilleros, families enjoying their evening aperitif and people simply relaxing around the equestrian statue of Felipe III. A little-known feature of the Plaza Mayor are the small bronze plaques set inconspicuously in the base of the street lamps. They tell the square's history, from executions and bullfights, to coronations and canonizations. There is even one dedicated to Enrique Tierno Galván, who served as mayor from 1979 to 1986 and is widely acknowledged as the most popular incumbent in Madrid's history. After three devastating fires and half a dozen name changes, the

Plaza Mayor, with Casa de la Panadería.

Plaza Mayor as it stands today was completed in 1854. Mercifully, none of the structure has been touched by the developer's wrecking ball. One of the most striking original features is the Casa de la Panadería (Bakery House), with its Flemish-style towers and spires, which now houses the Madrid tourism bureau.

The Plaza Mayor is a matchless setting from which to contemplate the ebb and flow of Madrid life, the only possible exception being the upstairs window table at the Mallorquina café in the Puerta del Sol, the city's hustle-and-bustle central square – should you be lucky enough to bag this coveted spot.

This fiercely sought-after belvedere in one of the city's most iconic plazas opens onto a vast panorama of Madrid history. The Puerta del Sol was the scene of the 1802 revolt against Napoleon's occupying troops, as well as the 1868 uprising that overthrew Queen Isabel II, the proclamation of the ill-fated Second Republic of 1931 and the start of the 2011 anti-austerity Indignados movement that spread from Madrid around the world. Looking left from the café window, the emblematic rooftop Tío Pepe Sherry hoarding tips its top hat to the pedestrianized (save for buses and taxis) streets below, while to the right, set into the pavement, the equally celebrated

Kilometre Zero brass plaque marks the point from which all major roads lead out of the city. It is set in front of the entrance to regional government's headquarters, where legend has it that when the building was under construction in the eighteenth century, the Devil appeared to warn that all those on the construction site would be condemned to eternal flames, as lackeys of a town council that chose the designs of a French architect over a Spanish one. The choice had come about as a clash of royal tastes. The celebrated architect Ventura Rodríguez was a favourite of King Fernando vi. The king's successor and half-brother, Carlos iii, was an admirer of Jacques Marquet, who worked extensively in Bourbon Spain. At the time of completion, a priest was brought in to join the team of builders, just in case the Devil chose to make a second appearance.

At the far end of the Puerta del Sol, at the start of the Calle de Alcalá, stands the 18-tonne statue of a bear nibbling at a strawberry tree, the symbol from Madrid's coat-of-arms. It is said that this image came about when King Alfonso vi's Christian army entered the Moorish settlement. The name suggested for the newly conquered town was Ursa, Latin for bear – in the eleventh century these

View of Puerta del Sol and the Tío Pepe sign.

animals roamed the nearby hills, large tracts of which were covered in strawberry trees.

From this spot, a short walk along Calle Mayor takes you to the spacious Plaza de Oriente, facing the grandiose Baroque-Classical Royal Palace, which is nearly twice the size of London's Buckingham Palace. Somewhere under the cobbles there runs a tunnel from the palace to the wine cellar at the early eighteenth-century Sobrino de Botín restaurant near the Plaza Mayor. This was used by King Alfonso XII as a passageway to meet his mistress, the opera singer Elena Sanz, at a secluded nook in what the Guinness Book of Records lists as the world's oldest existing restaurant.

Vying with the bear and strawberry tree for the title of Madrid's most venerated symbol is the Cibeles fountain in the Plaza de Cibeles. The statue rises at the northern end of a trio of fountains built in the eighteenth century to adorn the Paseo del Prado. A cloaked Apollo rises on a tall pedestal midway along the promenade, facing the Naval Museum, while Neptune stands astride his chariot in the Plaza de las Cortes, the home of the Spanish parliament. The Roman god was sculpted in marble in the eighteenth century by the renowned Spanish architect and artist Ventura Rodríguez;

The Bear and the Strawberry Tree: a symbol of Madrid, Puerta del Sol.

Plaza de Oriente in the 1950s.

however, the original bronze trident was replaced by a bronze spear after its theft in 1914. This was later rectified with the return of the trident to the god's hand. During the hunger years of the Civil War, a banner was placed on the statue which read, 'Feed me or take away my fork.' Before the advent of centralized water systems, the Cibeles fountain served a practical function as a filling point for the municipal water carriers, who distributed it around the city in goat-skin bags. The fountain faces what was once Europe's largest and most ornate post office, the Palacio de Comunicaciones. This building now houses Madrid's city hall, which shares the cathedral-like space with art galleries, eateries and, of course, the popular rooftop bar, with its magnificent night-time view of the city. The building's patio was described by the renowned Madrid architect Fernando Chueca Goitia as 'a true urban plaza'. Visitors can climb to the clock tower to marvel at the tiled walls surrounding the spiral staircase.

The pomposity of Spain's Habsburg and Bourbon monarchs is patently evident in the grandeur of Madrid's plazas. But not all conform to this display of royal narcissism. Many charming hideaways lie off the beaten track. The Plaza de la Cruz Verde was the city's main square before the Plaza Mayor was built. It is scarcely noticeable today, almost hidden behind the traffic-laden Calle de Segovia in the heart of the historic district of Habsburg Madrid. The name derives from the green cross that in 1680 presided over the last heretic burning on this spot. A short distance away is the Plaza de San Javier, Madrid's smallest square, which is enclosed on three sides by a single block of flats. It is an ancient site, where Islamic artefacts were discovered under the building's disused rubbish dump. In the nineteenth century, the legendary bandit Luis Candelas slipped into one of the houses to pay nocturnal visits to his lover.

Fiestas and Processions

'Madrid is the fiesta-mad capital of a country awash with religious and secular holidays. It is worth noting that France has fourteen public holidays a year, Germany nineteen and Italy 23. Spain rejoices in 41 official fiestas, with the greatest number of them celebrated in Madrid.

Should you happen to be strolling about central Madrid on the seventh day of December, you might look up and down the streets and wonder what's become of the city's 3.2 million inhabitants. The answer is that they are probably luxuriating on the beaches of Valencia or the Canary Islands, perhaps enjoying a short break in London or Paris, or simply escaping the winter cold in the comfort of their homes.

How has this come about in a city whose citizens delight in street life? Madrid has given the world a new meaning of the word 'bridge', or *puente* in Spanish. Constitution Day falls on 6 December and Immaculate Conception two days later, hence – with the exception of the hapless corps of wage earners running the city's public services – Madrileños see no point in going to work on the 'bridging' day between fiestas. But it gets worse – or better, depending on how one views the relative merits of labour versus leisure. If Constitution Day happens to fall on a Wednesday, with Friday of course also being a public holiday, the *puente* expands into an *acueducto*, and for five days Madrid becomes all but a ghost town.

But outward appearances can be deceptive. Those Madrileños who, by necessity or choice, have not joined the general exodus, are to be found revelling in the city's bars and taverns, which are almost

innumerable. To put this into perspective, locals will assure you that in the 685 metres (750 yards) separating Plaza de Antón Martín from Plaza de Tirso de Molina, there are to be found more bars than in all of Norway.

Madrid's festive tradition stretches back more than five hundred years. The city's first Corpus Christi procession took place in 1482, with a torch-bearing Queen Isabel of Castile leading a retinue of white-cassocked, chanting friars along the Calle Mayor. This celebration is held in late May or early June, starting at 7 p.m. when a cortège of military officers and ecclesiastical hierarchy, followed by a band playing liturgical music, departs the Almudena Cathedral to march along a route not much different from that followed by the Catholic queen.

There are several yearly festivals that never fail to send Madrileños flocking into the streets by the thousands. One of the liveliest and most *castizo* (traditional) is the fiesta of San Isidro, the city's patron saint. This festival can boast upwards of thirty events, starting about a week before the saint's day on 15 May and carrying on into early June. These are days and nights of almost non-stop concerts, shows, children's parties and much street dancing to the two-step of the *chotis*, a folk dance of Bohemian origin. A highlight is the mass picnic for families and friends in the park Pradera de San Isidro, after which there is a procession that winds through the city centre, with Madrileños in the traditional dress of Goya's time. After all, it was Goya who immortalized the May festivities in his 1788 painting *La pradera de San Isidro* (The Meadow of San Isidro). All are welcome to partake and many shops hire out fiesta costumes for ladies (*chulapas*), their heads bedecked with a white scarf and red carnation, showing off their flamboyant frocks and accompanied by dapper men (*chulapos*) in flat caps and chequered waistcoats, also sporting red carnations.

The Fiesta of Our Lady of the Almudena takes place on 9 November, in honour of Madrid's female patron saint. This is a solemn occasion in which women dressed in black, with mantillas

Traditional dancers at the festival of La Paloma in Lavapiés.

Holy week procession.

and combs to match, parade through the streets of Old Madrid behind a column of city dignitaries and the municipal band, leading the statue of the saint on a carriage. The name Almudena comes from the Arabic *al mudayna*, meaning citadel. Legend has it that at the time of the Moorish conquest of Madrid in the eighth century, the Christian inhabitants concealed an image of the saint in the fortress walls to protect it from the invaders. It was discovered by Madrid's liberator Alfonso VI, who found, moreover, that the two candles placed alongside her image some three centuries previous were still alight. In 1948 she was crowned patron saint of Madrid and on the morning of 9 November it is worth witnessing the spectacular Mass celebrated in the Almudena Cathedral. After the religious ceremony, the cathedral swiftly empties and there is a dash to the Plaza Mayor's bars for tapas and lunch.

By far one of Madrid's most dramatic events of the year is the Semana Santa, or Holy Week celebration. Since the fifteenth century, during this week religious icons have been taken from their normal resting places in churches and paraded through the streets on the shoulders of *costaleros*, mostly young men who consider themselves privileged to struggle under the immense weight of religious statues, balanced – sometimes rather precariously – on heavy platforms. In Madrid there are around twenty of these religious events over the days before Easter Sunday. The most emblematic is held on Good Friday, starting in the late evening and carrying on into the night, when a silent procession leaves the Church of Santísimo Cristo de la Fe in Calle Atocha, simultaneous with another from the Parish Church of Santa Cruz in the same street, carrying the image of Lignum Crucis. On this occasion the religious icons are borne by men in Ku Klux Klan-style costumes, to a background of sombre liturgical music. This bizarre outfit, called *capirote*, is worn by some brotherhoods as a symbol of penitence and long pre-dates the American Klan version, which was modelled on the Spanish religious attire.

The real test of endurance is the three-in-one non-stop fiesta, from 1 to 15 August, in honour of San Cayetano, San Lorenzo and the Virgen de la Paloma. The events are centred in the intensely *castizo* neighbourhoods of Lavapiés and La Latina, whose narrow, winding streets are garlanded with carnations and banners. The squares are bustling with food stalls: here is an opportunity to savour traditional fare, from churros with hot chocolate to roast hog. The partying is enlivened by traditional music and pop groups, street theatre and dancing into the night. The finale is the more subdued, though no less colourful, floral offering to the Virgen de la Paloma. The saint is held dear to the hearts of Madrileños, and following the solemn Mass celebrated in the church of the same name, her image is carried through the city's historic barrios, to the accompaniment of the municipal band.

An event not to be missed is the blessing of the animals on 17 January, in celebration of San Antón, the patron saint of animals. The origins of this event go back centuries to a ritual of pagan origin known as the festival of 'the king of hogs'. This was a race in what is now the Retiro Park, in which the winning swine was solemnly crowned and led in procession to a chapel in the park for a fête, which rather unfairly featured roast pig. When the chapel was demolished in 1760, a new tradition arose, the blessing of the animals

Blessing the animals, festival of San Antón.

at the Church of San Antón in Calle de Hortaleza. The street is closed to traffic all day from the morning, as people walk or carry their dogs, cats, canaries, tortoises, parrots and even fish past a street-level window, from which the parish priest anoints their heads with holy water. When we lifted our part-Alsatian to the window, we noticed several plasters on the priest's hand and wondered what lay in store for him with the woman behind us, who led a Vietnamese pot-bellied pig.

Café Society

On a wet Monday evening in May we arrive at the Gran Café Gijón, Paseo de Recoletos, 21. We are here for one of Madrid's unique café happenings, the *tertulia*. On Mondays the poets' *tertulia* gather to read, recite, chat, compare notes and argue about poetry. The Gijón is still very quiet at 9 p.m. and we wonder if we've come on the right night, but the head waiter, José Bárcena, who has been overseeing the group for more than thirty years, assures us that the *tertulia* will form. And sure enough they start drifting in, a mixture of men and women, mostly middle-aged, with a sprinkling of younger, arty, student-looking types in their twenties, then several well into retirement age, to a blind, 95-year-old veteran poet, accompanied by his South American carer. There is drinking, chat, laughter and much rummaging among papers until the first poet stands to read her poem, a meditation on changing times and time passing, to applause and shouted encouragement. From here on the *tertulia* is in full swing, as verses are read from notebooks and smart phones, to a highly dramatic recitation from memory of a poem that's obviously familiar to the group, by a man who looks like a retired sea captain. By 11 p.m. the poetry is still going strong. We are fading, so we walk back out into the rainy night as another animated burst of applause and chat livens up the café.

In starting to write this piece, we pondered 'What is the difference between a Madrid café and a bar, or patisserie, or even a restaurant?' They all have more similarities than differences: waiters serving alcoholic and non-alcoholic drinks, coffees and tapas. Many cafés also serve elaborate meals, in either the main space and/or in

Café Gijón.

a separate upstairs or downstairs restaurant. And yet, a true café is distinctly different, with people having their favourite, in which they may spend a great deal of time. Part of the café vibe is that it's OK to linger over your drink. It seems unthinkable that a waiter would be 'asking for the table back', even if there are other people sitting down to lunch or dinner. In the Gijón there are known tables, around the edge, away from the windows, if you just want to stop in for a drink during lunch or dinner service.

The novelist Benito Pérez Galdós describes the particular feeling for café life in nineteenth-century Madrid in his most famous novel, *Fortunata and Jacinta* (1887). His chapter 'The Café' begins:

> Juan Pablo Rubín didn't feel alive unless he spent half his day or almost all of it at the café . . . He went to the café after lunch, in the early afternoon, and stayed until four or five o'clock. After dinner, at about eight, he usually went back, and stayed until past midnight or daybreak, depending on the occasion.

Juan Pablo meets the same core group of friends each evening, forming their own *tertulia*:

> They occupied three tables that the waiter set up before they arrived . . . Juan Pablo entered slowly . . . and always sat in exactly the same place . . . he drew his glass nearer and put the sugar bowl on the right, at the discreet distance at which one places an inkwell when writing, and he watched the operation of pouring the milk and coffee into the glass, making quite sure that the proportion of these liquids were right and that the glass was filled just to the brim. This was essential . . . Being a veteran of the café, he knew how to have his coffee with that slowness and art that an important act demands.

Once the group of five friends are assembled their evening *tertulia* begins, always going over the politics of the day:

> Since they all had the same mania, each one cultivated a speciality; Leopoldo Montes brought news of a political turnover almost every day; Don Basilio always had gossip about bureaucratic issues; Relimpio was precocious and malicious in his judgements; Rubín stood out for thinking he knew everything and could forecast events; and, finally, Feijóo was profoundly sceptical and took all politics with a grain of salt.

José Gutiérrez Solana, *La tertulia del café de Pombo*, 1920, oil on canvas.

The *tertulia* tradition began in the eighteenth century in private houses, in a similar fashion to the Paris 'salon' where the notables of the day would meet to discuss politics, with the *tertulia* often having a particular political allegiance. By the early nineteenth century, the appeal and membership of *tertulias* had broadened considerably, moving into the public space with informal and semi-formal groups gathering on a daily basis in Madrid's many cafés. The famous painting of 1920 by José Gutiérrez Solana, *La tertulia del café de Pombo* (The Gathering at the Café de Pombo), in his unique expressionist style, can be seen today in the Reina Sofía Museum. It is the artist's most iconic work, expressing his enjoyment of these intellectual gatherings, which were more popular than ever in the early decades of the twentieth century. The picture was donated to the nation in 1947 by Ramón Gómez de la Serna, the central standing figure in the group depicted, which also comprises some of the most notable intellectuals of the period: Manuel Abril, Tomás Borrás, José Bergamín, José Cabrero, Mauricio Bacarisse, Solana in self-portrait,

Pedro Emilio Coll and Salvador Bartolozzi. Alas, the nineteenth-century Café Pombo is no longer open in the Calle Carretas, but a new Café Pombo Sagrada Cripta is open in the building where Ramón Gómez de la Serna used to live, on Calle Guillermo Rolland, 7. He was the founder of the Saturday night *tertulia* called 'La sagrada cripta del Pombo', hence the name of the new café.

There are also more modern takes on the *tertulia*. For example, the Intruso Bar on Calle de Augusto Figueroa has a broad programme of artistic events, including fusion music concerts on Mondays and jazz on Tuesdays, and the monthly 'Madrid Poetry Slam' in which twelve poets each have a three-minute slot and the patrons vote for the winner.

The recent history of the Café Comercial (at Glorieta de Bilbao, 7) illustrates the loyalty and affection which a great café generates. El Comercial opened in 1887 and rapidly became popular as a place for the writers of the day to congregate, including the poet Antonio Machado, author of the poem 'On the Banks of the Duero' (1907), the Nobel Prize-winning playwright Jacinto Benavente and the writer Camilo José Cela, also a winner of the Nobel Prize in Literature, who was inspired by the café to write 'The Hive' (1950). The café closed in July 2015, to the dismay of its loyal customers. The shuttered doors and walls were plastered with affectionate messages and anecdotes from patrons. After standing shut for two years, it re-opened in 2017, with a full refurbishment that has retained its former glory of marble counters, heavy velvet furnishings and original light fittings.

The Café Comercial is central to Cela's 'The Hive', set in 1942 around the daily existence of the café's patrons, including a musician, a mediocre non-conformist poet, a kind-hearted money lender, a black-marketeer's bookkeeper and an assortment of prostitutes, singers and seducers. Doña Rosa tyrannizes her waiters and customers alike and Cela shows little sympathy for the unpleasant café owner and her expensive tastes: 'she smokes cigarettes at ninety centimes the packet, and from the moment she gets up to the moment she goes to bed, she drinks Ojén anis, whole glasses full of the best.'

On a lighter note, the songwriter Marcial Guareño wrote a poem about the café, which was set to music by Alfonso Muñoz: 'Si quiere usted tomar un café rico, acuda al Comercial que es exquisito' (If you want to have a superb coffee, go to the Comercial, which is exquisite). There is a revival of the relaxed café-bar in areas like La Latina and Malasaña. The traditional Café del Nuncio at Calle Segovia, 9, has been taken over and given a makeover by the Café Angélica company, which is very serious about the quality of its coffee, with a number of different roasts and blends, so the coffee is better than ever. What it has lost in 'atmosphere' is amply compensated for by its new stylish appearance. The café now serves a range of vermouths and cocktails, tapas and cakes in a decidedly lighter and brighter interior than the fusty, dusty red velvet and dark green paintwork of yesteryear. Malasaña offers the range of cafés, including new-style literary experience of the bookshop-cum-café at Vergüenza Ajena, Galileo, 56, which holds literary events including invited readings by poets for 'poetry jams without embarrassment' (*vergüenza*). On a similar theme there is J&J Books and

Coffee and churros at Café Comercial.

Jazz at Café Central.

Coffee, Calle Espiritu Santo, 47, which is more a New York-style coffee shop than a traditional café.

The Chueca district has seen new retro-style cafés open which maintain the old feel of the café as a place to drop in and linger. Our favourite is Café de la Luz at Calle Puebla, 8 (presumably named after the numerous specialist light shops in the street, which offer an array of retro and new styles, plus repairs and spare mantles for lights and lamps). The café has a delightful cosy-kitsch interior with sofas, comfy chairs and shelves piled with old books and magazines. Traditional places along the Paseo de Recoletos in central Madrid, the Gijón and the Espejo (not that old in years but still traditional in style) have wonderful summer *terrazas*, which offer a cooler, relaxed place to sit and people-watch the strollers along the paseo. All this accompanied, in the case of the Gijon, by a pianist at a grand piano, who applauds with the patrons of the café after every number.

So many cafés to choose from but, while we may dabble in trying traditional and 'new kids on the block' cafés in different locations, I know that we will always end up back at the Gijón – it's our place.

In its day, the Gijón hosted Federico García Lorca and Pablo Neruda and is still popular with artists, writers and actors, including Carmen Maura, Rosa Montero, José Ovejero and Arturo Pérez-Reverte. As Pérez Galdós reflects: 'The café is like a grand fair where countless products of the human mind are bought and sold. Naturally there are more trinkets than anything else; but in their midst, and sometimes going unnoticed, there are priceless gems.'

Football Madness

King Alfonso XIII reached his majority in 1902, and took over the monarchy from his mother, the regent María Cristina. Like a great number of sixteen-year-old Madrileños, Alfonso was an avid fan of a sport recently imported from England, called football. The king soon became a regular spectator at matches of the Madrid Football Club, founded in the year he ascended the throne. Alfonso was in fact such an enthusiast of the club that in 1920 he bestowed on it the title of real (royal), together with the royal crown that today adorns the Real Madrid emblem.

The king might well have taken pride in the new Madrid club, which would in the coming decades set a football record by winning nine European cups. Real Madrid has chalked up so vast an array of trophies – to date, thirteen European cups, seven Club World Cup championships, more than thirty La Liga championships and close to twenty Copas del Rey – it was almost inevitable that in 2000 the club was awarded the title of best club of the twentieth century in a FIFA poll.

Small wonder that on Real Madrid match days central Madrid is virtually taken over by thousands of noisy fans who pile into the city's bars, before and after the game, for drinks and a meal. Do not be surprised to hear cheering in a cacophony of languages, for this is more than a team – it is a sporting phenomenon that attracts football addicts from countries across Europe.

The iconic Cibeles Fountain that adorns the middle of a roundabout linking four of Madrid's main arteries is surrounded by chanting, singing Madridistas, unyielding to the swarm of cars and buses struggling to get past the crowds. Traffic on the broad, tree-lined Paseo de la Castellana, which bisects the city on a north–south axis, is brought to a standstill at Real Madrid's Santiago Bernabéu Stadium. The 70,000-seater sports ground was named after the stocky forward with a keen eye for goals, the man who was team president from 1943 to his death in 1978. To Bernabéu goes much of the credit for transforming Real Madrid into what it is today, the most successful football club in Europe, with annual revenues of nearly £700 million.

Real Madrid is undoubtedly the city's star team, but it is not the only show in town. Within twenty years of its founding, two more professional teams came on the scene: Atlético Madrid and Rayo Vallecano. El Atleti, as it is affectionately known to fans, was founded one morning in 1903 at the Basque-Navarre Club in Madrid's very *castizo* Calle de la Cruz in 1903. Atlético came into being as what might be called an anti-Real Madrid club. The team was put together by a group of Basque students who had considered the play of

Fan merchandise outside the Bernabéu stadium.

The Santiago Bernabéu stadium, home of Real Madrid.

Madrid FC (which would become Real Madrid) so ungentlemanly that they vowed to form their own club. This club grew and grew, becoming the second largest in the city and the rivalry with Real Madrid was born.

Atlético's shining moment came immediately after the 1936–9 Spanish Civil War. Before 1939 the team had not been a major player in Spanish football. When they formed a link with the Spanish Air Force's team, which had started playing during the Civil War, they soon became one of the stronger teams in the first post-war season of 1939/40. At a time when many other clubs were struggling just to remain in existence, this partnership with the military helped Atlético to win the La Liga title of 1939/40, a complete turnaround from having finished second bottom in 1935/6. Alas, the team's presidential elections of 1987 were won by right-wing demagogue Jesús Gil – the future mayor of Marbella, the Costa del Sol resort town

Real Madrid playing Atlético Madrid, 7 November 2010.

which became a haven for British, Italian and Russian gangsters. During the Franco years it was also a playground for Nazis like Otto Remer and Léon Degrelle, who had fled to Spain to avoid prosecution for war crimes. Gil's mismanagement of Atlético left the club's finances in a parlous state and got the team relegated in the 1999/2000 season. It was not until former player Diego Simeone's arrival as coach in 2011 that the picture began to brighten. Simeone and his cut-above-the-rest coaching brought results and prize money, which led to even better results and even more prize money, a simplified formula that nonetheless explains the club's recent sporting and financial success.

Atlético's match days are celebrated at the Neptune Fountain in the Paseo del Prado, close to Parliament and the Prado Museum. Real Madrid is unquestionably the aristocrat of Spanish football, while Atlético Madrid is perceived as the hero of the city's working classes. This is reflected in their home stadium. The Bernabéu stands majestically astride the sedate northern quarter of middle-class Madrid, while Atlético until recently had to make do with the rather rundown Vicente Calderón in the blue-collar Arganzuela district to the south. Likewise, megastar Real Madrid's pockets are at least four times deeper than Atlético's, which recently found itself in financial straits over its new Metropolitano Stadium. The grounds are known as Wanda Metropolitano for sponsorship reasons, while fans have nicknamed it La Peineta, the traditional Spanish ladies' comb, for its convex design. It stands in San Blas, on the other side of the city. It may seem ironic that Atlético, supposedly the club of the working class, counts among its loyal fans no lesser a personage than King Felipe VI. One wonders what Alfonso XIII would have made of his great-grandson's team loyalty.

An entertaining way of exploring the history of the two big clubs is on a visit to their stadiums. Real Madrid offers a tour of the Santiago Bernabéu Stadium, which is startling for the size of the structure it reveals. The tour starts with a look at the Presidential box and a visit to the team's changing rooms. After this, visitors can follow in the players' footsteps through the tunnel, out onto the edge of the pitch. The experience is topped off with a visit to the trophy museum and its dazzling display of the hundreds of cups that Real Madrid has won in its more than one-hundred-year career. If you choose to do the tour without a guide, you will be given a guide-book in English and Spanish and will simply need to follow the

Inauguration of the new stadium of Atlético Madrid, Wanda Metropolitano, on 16 September 2017.

yellow arrows. The Real Madrid Museum contains a wealth of written history about the club, as well as a wall covered with photos and trophies galore. Not to be outdone, Atlético also offers fans and visitors a tour of its new stadium, which takes you through the players' tunnel, the pitch, stands, auditorium and the dressing rooms.

The third of Madrid's best-known clubs made its debut in 1924, with the founding of Rayo Vallecano (there are, in fact, five Madrid teams in the Spanish La Liga, the two lesser-known clubs being Getafe and Leganés, each with their own stadium and fan base). The Vallecas stadium lies in the heart of what was at the time of the team's creation a suburban township. Once half a day's journey from the centre of Madrid, the heart of Vallecas is now less than half an hour on the Metro to Portazgo station. This is a self-consciously trendy, quirky blue-collar neighbourhood, radiating a cheerful blend of heavy metal music and hardcore leftism. The Vallecanos (the ultra-hip spell it with a 'k' to accentuate the trendiness) are proud of their lower-class origins, and the football team that embodies their turf. Some look down their noses at Atlético as a pseudo working-class club, but there is no question of Rayo's proletarian credentials. Rayo Vallecano are as much a social phenomenon as a football club.

Theatre

Spain's transition to democracy after the death of Franco in 1975 brought a new flourishing of theatre to Madrid, a city whose theatre tradition can be traced back five centuries. The latest trend is in alternative productions performed in small venues, usually combined with café-theatres, dance spaces and galleries. Fancy stopping in for fifteen minutes or so of theatre entertainment before or after dinner? On a Saturday evening Madrid's 'Microtheatre' is the face of post-recession Spain. The venue offers 54 mini-shows back-to-back in a block of flats in the stylish Malasaña district. Breaking through the café chatter, a voice calls the audience downstairs to a basement auditorium that seats a dozen or so spectators. Punters can choose from a range of fifteen-minute plays, from a comedy staged in a 1960s Spanish kitchen to dark drama set in a medieval torture chamber. For the admission price of €4, this theatre is hard to beat in value for money. La Escalera de Jacob, in the heart of the historic Lavapiés district, is another of Madrid's small and friendly theatre-bars, featuring stand-up comedy in English and some Spanish. The audience is invited to participate in a confidential conversation with the actors on stage, which results in a hilarious feel-good Friday frolic. If you happen to be visiting with a family, children's plays are regularly put on at the Sala la Bicicleta in Madrid's sprawling Casa de Campo park. The weekly Guía del Ocio usually carries a listing of English-language plays.

In 1561 Madrid acquired upwards of 7,000 new citizens, nearly doubling the city's population overnight. These were the grandees, the high-born, members of the military hierarchy and assorted

Teatro Español.

hangers-on at court who were part of King Felipe II's entourage on the march from Toledo to his new capital. Compared with the sumptuous city the monarch had left behind, Madrid was in those days an outpost of little distinction, perched high on the barren Castilian plateau.

As early as the first century BC, Toledo had won the praises of the Roman historian Livy, while in the twelfth century AD scholars travelled from all parts of Europe to study Latin translations of Arabic reworkings of Greek philosophy and science. Madrid was, by comparison, a cultural wasteland. The new arrivals suffered from ennui, a lack of courtly diversions. They longed for entertainment to help them cope with the harsh living conditions of their new abode.

In short order, theatre came on the scene to provide amusement for a bored elite, as well as the ordinary citizenry, the latter of course safely segregated from the privileged classes. The precursors of the city's theatres were the *corrales*. These were custom-built municipal venues, established in rectangular courtyards, overlooked by the backs of houses whose windows served as viewing boxes. The first of the *corrales*, El Corral de la Cruz, was opened as early as 1597, followed in quick succession by El Corral del Príncipe. The Teatro Español, the direct descendant of the Corral del Príncipe, still stands today in the Calle del Príncipe, behind the Plaza de Santa Ana. Most of the plays staged in these two theatres were translations of popular French works. Both venues were sombre and comfortless, with ladies seated separately in the balcony. In place of gas footlights to illuminate the stage, as existed in Paris or London theatres, lighting was provided by a large candelabra mounted overhead.

The social profile of seventeenth-century theatre fans represented the highest echelons of Madrid society. Suffice it to point out that King Felipe IV, who ruled from 1621 to 1640, was a regular attendee at the comedies and religious plays staged at the Corral de la Cruz. The theatre was located in Calle de la Cruz, a few minutes' stroll from the Puerta del Sol. The last but one of Spain's Habsburg monarchs was particularly drawn to performances which featured Madrid's leading female actress of the day, María Calderón. This stage diva became Felipe's lover, an affair that produced an illegitimate

Teatro de la Zarzuela.

son, Juan José de Austria, who rose to become commander-in-chief of the Spanish army.

The French diplomat Antoine de Brunel visited Madrid in the heyday of the city's seventeenth-century Golden Age of literature. He noted in his travel memoirs the Madrileños' passion for the stage. 'It is almost impossible to find a seat in the city's two official theatres [*corrales*],' he wrote. 'The most distinguished members of society buy their tickets in advance . . . even in Paris, where plays are put on every day, the turnout is not so overwhelming.'

This was the age of Spain's great dramatists – Lope Félix de Vega, Tirso de Molina, Pedro Calderón de la Barca and Juan Ruiz de Alarcón, among others – all of whom wrote and lived in, or adjacent to, Madrid's literary quarter, the Barrio de las Letras. They were a community of boisterous and eccentric characters. Lope himself would attend stage performances at one of the *corrales* to flirt with the women who, by municipal ordinance, were crowded into the balcony. On other occasions, he would turn up to watch performances of plays by his rival Tirso de Molina, equipped with a handful of tomatoes to hurl at the stage.

For more than 150 years, the *corrales* continued to pack in the crowds, leading to a growing number of venues, many of which were covered auditoriums that would be recognizable today as proper theatres. With the arrival of the Bourbon dynasty in 1621, theatre culture became more accessible to Madrid's fast-growing population. A number of the city's most opulent corners were adapted to host drama. These included salons of the nobility's sumptuous stately homes and the Sabatini Gardens of the Royal Palace, still a magical setting for outdoor evening performances of classical drama and opera.

But it was in the nineteenth century that Madrid experienced the biggest growth in the number of theatres of its history. Between 1839 and 1897, 28 new theatres opened their doors in a city of fewer than 500,000 inhabitants. The public could choose from a variety of productions, from Lope de Vega classics to zarzuela. This latter genre of light-hearted operetta à la Gilbert and Sullivan remains one of Madrid's most characteristic and best-loved forms of entertainment. The Teatro de la Zarzuela opened in 1856, on the birthday of Queen Isabel II, and soon became the rendezvous for Spanish light-opera aficionados. The spectacular costumes and dancing make this an exhilarating experience, which the non-Spanish speaker can follow in the English-language plot summaries available at performances of major works. From October to June, zarzuela fans can enjoy a repertoire of works depicting everyday Spanish scenes, accompanied by popular tunes.

The Rastro flea market in the 1950s.

Markets

In his autobiography *The Forging of a Rebel* the writer and journalist Arturo Barea describes the Rastro flea market from around 1910. At this time, the streets on either side of the Ribera de Curtidores still housed the tanneries that gave the road its name, and their smell pervaded the market: 'an acrid smell of rotting flesh, which fills the whole quarter and clutches at your throat. On that slope the street hawkers set up their stalls and you can buy everything, except what you set out to buy.'

The Rastro is Madrid's most famous market. It is still held on Sundays and Bank holidays from 9.00 a.m. to 3.00 p.m., spreading from the Plaza de Cascorro, down the Calle de la Ribera de Curtidores to the Ronda de Toledo, taking in the side streets along the way. Like many traditional flea markets these days, the Rastro now has a lot of stalls selling ubiquitous 'market goods': cheap T-shirts, leggings, Indian scarves, knock-off bags and trainers, together with tourist trinkets, which group together to sell particular types of goods. However, there are still some traditional stalls. For example, along the so-called Calle de los Pájaros (Bird Street), in Calle de Fray Ceferino González, there are still caged bids and bird seed for sale, as well as other pet supplies; similarly, Calle San Cayetano, known as the street of the painters, still has shops and stalls selling paintings, drawings and art supplies. The further in you go along the side streets, the more fascinating the market becomes. There are stalls specializing in second-hand comic books, coins and stamps, as well as the true flea-market mix of stalls, with grotty broken bits and pieces of kitchen equipment

79 Shopping for hats at the Rastro.

and crockery, alongside serious antiques traders. Barea describes going to the market, as a boy of around twelve, to buy pieces of old metal to build a toy steam engine:

> There they sell every used thing people get rid of. There are old clothes worn out fifty years ago . . . dented musical instruments, pots and pans of all sizes, rusty surgical knives, old bicycles with twisted wheels, absurd clocks . . . and old iron. A great deal of old iron: twisted bars . . . hoops, pipes, heavy pieces of machinery, monstrous cog wheels . . . anvils with blunted noses, coils of wire covered in ochre rust, and tools. There are hundreds of stalls and thousands of people looking and buying. All Madrid walks about the Rastro on Sunday mornings . . . Little by little my steam engine was born out of it.

At the bottom of the Calle de la Ribera, Gypsy antique dealers set up their stalls with a misleadingly jumbled and careless appearance. What can at first glance seem like unfashionable ornaments and bric-à-brac turn out to be valuable *objets d'art*, such as an exquisite bunch of glass grapes, which we thought had 'retro charm', until we noticed the price of €1,800 (over £1,500).

Apart from the famous flea market, Madrid's traditional food markets continue to go strong, with refurbished buildings and the reinvention of the market experience once again putting them ahead of the supermarket as the fashionable place for food shopping. The first covered markets were built in the 1830s and continued to play a vital role in shopping for the next 150 years before declining as the twentieth century drew to a close. Now, as the traditional local markets receive makeovers, they provide a great way to get to know the personalities of different neighbourhoods – from the posh area of Salamanca, with its market selling traditional conserves and foie gras, to the bohemian Lavapiés, where the market features organic produce and craft beers. Across the city, market stalls showcase every type of regional and more exotic delicacies, while the stallholders and shoppers reveal the passion that accompanies shopping, cooking and eating in Madrid.

The place that in many ways started the markets' renaissance is the Mercado de San Miguel, close to the Plaza Mayor, built in 1916 and more or less abandoned by the end of the century, before re-opening in 2009 after extensive renovation. The building is a gem, the only market still with its original wrought iron and glass structure intact. Thanks to its location, it is now 'tourist central'. While the quality of the food on offer is high (such as seafood pinchos, freshly-cooked pimientos de Padrón and a great range of sherries), it's all about eating here and now – the majority of the thirty-plus stalls sell ready-to-eat tapas – rather than being somewhere for serious cooks to source ingredients. To shop in a less crowded venue, with more opportunity to have a good look (and smell) of the produce before buying, there is good reason to venture into some of the other central neighbourhood markets.

The Mercado de San Antón in the Chueca district, just north of the Gran Vía, was the second traditional neighbourhood market to get the makeover treatment. Not nearly so picturesque as San Miguel, this market is housed in a modern four-storey brick building. It has the advantage of space and light, so it doesn't feel as overwhelming as Mercado de San Miguel can when it's packed. Mercado de San Antón really combines the best of all (foodie) worlds: 'sensible food' shopping is catered for in the ground-floor supermarket; fresh, high-quality and exotic food fills the first-floor market stalls, including a beautiful array of fruits and legumes, fresh fish and meat, cured meats – not least a wonderful selection of Serrano ham – and regional cheeses. Moving up to the second floor, there are stalls with prepared foods, featuring favourite Spanish tapas, Italian delicacies, Japanese dishes and Asian street food. The stalls are arranged around the balcony overlooking the produce stalls, with tables and counters to eat at. The top floor houses a restaurant and bar with a large roof terrace, comfortable seating, music and views across the city. The restaurant menu heavily features Serrano ham and is popular with groups celebrating birthdays and anniversaries.

La Paz market has been catering to the bourgeois Salamanca district for well over a century. It can be found tucked away at the Paseo de la Castellana end of Calle de Ayala. This market, not so large as some of the others, has not needed to 'reinvent itself'; it just continues to provide the highest quality fresh food to the neighbourhood's well-heeled. It has, however, latched onto the idea of the market as a destination in its own right, with 'gourmet night' events which include tastings, cookery demonstrations and prize competitions for shoppers. There is also the innovation of the Amazon home delivery service at a couple of the stalls, with operators taking online orders and dispatching them by motorbike around the district and beyond.

Close to La Paz is 'Platea' in Calle Goya, still in the Salamanca district. This is a celebration of gastronomy in a different style. It is housed in the former Carlos III cinema and the genius has been not to do much conversion to the building, keeping an atmosphere of Hollywood golden-era glamour. The stage has been retained, as have the sweeping balconies, which now have restaurant tables from where you can survey Madrid's smart set eating and drinking on the lower floors at a range of bars and food stalls. The floors are themed by the food style: international cuisine on the lower ground floor; fresh produce stalls, traditional cheeses, Spanish wines and tapas on the ground floor, with lounges and a cocktail bar in what would

Mercado de San Miguel at night.

Serrano ham and cheese for sale in the Mercado de San Antón.

have been the 'circle', with the top balcony a restaurant specializing in Spanish-Peruvian fusion dishes. Overseeing the enterprise are three top chefs, Pepe Solla, Marcós Morán and Paco Roncero, with six Michelin stars between them.

Similar in that it is somewhere to hang out and have a drink and a snack, rather than buying the weekly food shop, is San Idelfonso market. It is completely different in character, self-consciously bohemian and verging on the achingly hip. The market is housed in a three-storey building on the site of an old market that was demolished in the 1970s. There are food stalls and bars across three floors, selling a mix of traditional and more exotic snacks, including tortilla, seafood, chorizo and truffle-flavoured steak tartare, with a pretty patio bar on the top floor. The kitsch decor and cool music all add to the atmosphere.

One of our favourite markets is the completely unpretentious Mercado de la Cebada in La Latina district's Plaza de la Cebada. It was originally a street market near the Puerta de Toledo, where farmers from the surrounding countryside would bring in their produce and set up informal stalls. In the nineteenth century a magnificent wrought iron and glass market building was opened, but this was hard to maintain and was replaced in the mid-twentieth century by the market's current home, a more prosaic warehouse-style building. This is the place to come for food shopping, as the produce is high quality but no frills. The fruit and vegetables, meat and fish are as good as those in the high-end locations. There are several newer stalls selling craft beers and Latin American specialities, adding a more modern feel, and it is conveniently also a place where you can get shoes and watches repaired. The market is going with the trends in a subtle way, having more stalls selling snacks to eat *in situ* on Saturday mornings, especially seafood stalls. The Mercado de la Cebada manages to balance tradition and utility with the modern 'market as food festival' approach.

Inside the Prado Museum.

Picture This

'Madrid is a great global capital, which today plays a leading role in the contemporary art scene' exclaims Patrizia Sandretto Re Rebaudengo, the celebrated Italian collector of contemporary art who professes her love for the city she calls her 'second homeland'. With the imminent opening of a dedicated gallery space in Madrid's old slaughterhouse on the Manazares River, the city will soon also be a home to a major part of her collection.

Madrid's long-term reputation as an art lover's destination has been firmly secured in the last twenty years, as the Prado Museum was joined by the Reina Sofía museum, housing the national collection of twentieth-century modern art, together with the establishment of the Thyssen-Bornemisza museum. This 'Golden Triangle' of art is the focal point for many a weekend-break in the capital.

The Prado is one of the longest-established public art galleries in the world and enormously important in Madrid's cultural development over the past two centuries. At its heart is the Royal Collection of around 3,000 paintings from the many royal palaces, together with the Museo de la Trinidad collection, which consisted of artworks requisitioned from monasteries and convents, many of which were closed down through a succession of government decrees in the nineteenth century. The establishment of the Prado as an art gallery is partly due to changing fashions in interior design. Fernando VII's queen, Isabel of Braganza, wanted rooms in the new Royal Palace to be wallpapered in the 'French style'. The Old Masters did not 'fit' with the fashionable look, so they were removed and stacked in corridors and attics around the palace. Perhaps after someone tripped over a painting for the fiftieth time, a decision was made to found an art museum in a nearby building which Carlos III had intended to establish as a natural history museum, but which had been damaged during the war with the French and left empty. The Royal Museum of Paintings and Sculptures was opened in 1819.

The museum survived political upheavals of the nineteenth and early twentieth centuries but was neglected during the Franco years. This chronic underfunding continued to the 1990s, when it was discovered that water was leaking through the roof and down the walls next to Velázquez's masterwork *Las Meninas*. Emergency repairs were carried out to the building. This was followed by extensive remodelling; raising the attic roof to create a new gallery floor, moving out all the offices to a nearby block and adding an extension joining the museum to the old cloisters of the Los Jerónimos monastery, to accommodate its growing collection and the explosion in visitor numbers. Even so, fewer than half of the museum's 7,000 works are on display at any one time. Perennially on display are masterpieces by Titian, Botticelli and Raphael, works by El Greco spanning three rooms, as well as canvases by Murillo, Claudio Coello and fine examples of Rubens. In addition to the treasures of the permanent collection, the museum mounts major temporary exhibitions throughout the year, many of which sell out. These have included showings of artists who until the twentieth century may not have been widely acknowledged, such as Hieronymus Bosch, a favourite of Felipe II, whose collection of works by the painter formed the heart of the exhibition.

The stars of the permanent collection at the Prado are undoubtedly Goya and Velázquez. The Goya works include his royal portraits, showing the nineteenth-century Bourbons in all their plump ungainliness, together with his paintings chronicling the stark violence of the Madrid uprising against the French and the 'black paintings' transferred from the walls of his home by the Manzanares River. The Prado holds many royal portraits by Velázquez, of Felipe IV, his queens and the baby princes who did not survive to adulthood, as well as the dramatic *Surrender of Breda* (1635) and the mythological *Triumph of Bacchus* (1628).

Las Meninas is considered such a priceless piece of art that it is the only painting never to accompany a Velázquez exhibition outside the museum – the insurance premiums alone would be prohibitive. The identities of those depicted in the painting are known from court records, but there are many interpretations of what is taking place on the canvas. The figures of the Velázquez *meninas* – the ladies in waiting, with their wide-hipped court dresses and wedges of hair – are immediately recognizable, iconic images, endlessly reproduced in modern paintings, prints, cards and ceramics. The *meninas* featured in a street art exhibition across Madrid in the summer of 2018 with eighty oversized statues of them placed in squares, parks and streets, each decorated by leading personalities from the worlds of Spanish culture, art, design and fashion. The organizers described the event as 'helping to reveal Velázquez's infinite message'.

At the end of the twentieth century the Prado was joined by the Museo Nacional Centro de Arte Reina Sofía, in the converted Hospital General de San Carlos by architect Francesco Sabatini, completed in 1778. The huge scale of the rooms in their austere style of stone and marble must have been less than cosy for the hospital's patients, but they make for a cool and neutral setting to display the museum's permanent collection of twentieth-century modern art, featuring works by Pablo Picasso, Joan Miró, Salvador Dalí and Juan Gris. The restyling of the hospital was enlivened by the addition of exterior glass lifts which make a striking contrast to the monumental severity of the Neoclassical building. With its huge gallery space the museum is able to constantly complement its permanent collection with a major programme of temporary exhibitions. These have been expanded in recent years through the addition of a dedicated space for temporary exhibitions, plus a library, restaurant and offices in three glass, terraced buildings around a courtyard to the west of the main building. The Reina Sofía's most famous holding is Pablo Picasso's monumental *Guernica*, the artist's powerful political statement depicting the bombing of the Basque town during the Spanish Civil War, painted for the Spanish Pavilion at the 1937 Paris World Fair.

The Caixa Forum gallery.

The Golden Triangle is completed by the Museo Thyssen-Bornemisza, housed in the charming Palacio de Villahermosa in the Paseo del Prado. This houses the former collection of Baron Hans Heinrich Thyssen-Bournemisza, who was persuaded by his (Spanish) wife, Carmen Cervera, to sell his family collection to the Spanish state for a nominal price. The collection covers all the major movements of European art with classic examples of each genre. The baron was particularly interested in Impressionism, post-Impressionism and post-war European and American art, so the collection has outstanding pieces from these movements. The gallery has been expanded since 2014 by the addition of two hundred paintings from Carmen Cervera's private collection. The Thyssen-Bornemisza also puts on magnificent temporary shows, with a particular focus on late nineteenth- and early twentieth-century artists: Paul Gauguin, Edvard Munch and Raoul Dufy have all been featured in masterfully curated exhibitions.

The 'big three' are joined by numerous smaller museums with interesting collections, contemporary galleries and art centres showing temporary exhibitions, so there is always something new to see on the art scene. Some of the most interesting shows are put on by business-related foundations. These include La Caixa Forum, Fundación MAPFRE and the Espacio Fundación Telefónica, which have benefited from government incentives for corporations to invest in social projects and in turn have given a boost to the visual arts.

La Caixa Forum is the largest of these foundations, with a total budget of €520 million in 2018 (£460 million). While 62 per cent of this went towards projects tackling social exclusion and poverty, there was still a sizeable fund available for the environment, science and cultural programmes. The foundation runs cultural spaces in many Spanish cities. Its showcase space in Madrid, Caixa Forum, lies on the Paseo del Prado, between the Reina Sofía Museum and the Prado. The forum has three exhibition spaces and a constantly changing programme of temporary exhibitions, which include art, photography and occasionally archaeology. In 2012 La Caixa Forum curated a major exhibition 'Before the Flood – Mesopotamia 3500–2100 BC' which brought together more than four hundred Mesopotamian objects from 32 museums and collections all over the world. The Forum has put on some imaginative exhibits, such as that featuring the artist, designer and would-be architect Giovanni Battista Piranesi (1720–1778). Piranesi's fanciful objects are more ornate than the most Rococo of taste could desire; a golden seashell-shaped grotto chair; a silver teapot, with a tortoise for the base, shells to form the pot and lid and a bee for the spout. They only ever existed as designs on paper until Factum Arte Madrid brought them to life with the miracle of 3D printing.

Since 2008 Fundación MAPFRE has put on an impressive programme of exhibitions, including Edward Hopper paintings, photography and even fashion (a wonderful Yves Saint Laurent retrospective) at its gallery on Paseo de Recoletos. This space has now been extended to include a permanent exhibition of works by Miró, and in 2014 the foundation also opened a gallery dedicated to photography, at the Bárbara de Braganza exhibition hall, a little further up the Paseo de Recoletos.

The Fundación Telefónica has converted the iconic Telefónica Building in the Grand Vía, the first skyscraper in Europe, into a four-floor exhibition space with a focus on mass communication and

The Matadero cultural centre.

technological media. It embodies the foundation's mission to educate people about the integration of technology, creativity and society. It presents excellent photography exhibitions along with shows at the boundaries of technology and art, with a focus on film, virtual reality and social media, but also looking to areas such as architecture, robotics and even space exploration.

In the 1990s, Spain launched an ambitious programme to convert major public buildings no longer required for their original purpose into art and cultural centres. Madrid has been at the forefront of this initiative in Spain, as was the case with the old post office, the sumptuous neo-Churrigueresque Palacio de Comunicaciones. Inaugurated in 1919, it is now known as the Palacio de Cibeles, home of the Madrid city council and the 'Centro-Centro' art gallery. The Centro Cultural Conde Duque has transformed an old army barracks, the headquarters of the elite Royal Guard, into a major cultural centre. It features a theatre, auditorium, temporary exhibition spaces and, in the summer, the courtyard becomes a open-air cinema and theatre. The building also houses the Museum of Contemporary Art, which has a growing collection of works by, mostly Spanish, established and new artists. One of the most fascinating exhibits in the museum is a re-creation of the avant-garde writer Ramón Gómez de la Serna's study, with reproductions of his collages, objects bought at Madrid's Rastro Sunday flea market, a wall of mirrors and artworks by his friends.

The most ambitious of these building transformations has been the conversion of the city's main slaughterhouse, the Matadero, by the Manzanares river, into a huge cultural centre. The building is vast and has yet to settle into a final form. There are already spaces for concerts, workshops, films and exhibitions. There is also a large plaza for markets and festivals, with a contemporary design market held the first weekend of the month, to showcase talented Spanish designers, artists and illustrators, where more than three hundred artists have shown their work. A huge 165,415-square-metre (1.8 million-sq.-ft) gallery space in the 'Nave 9' building at the Matadero displays radical contemporary art on loan from the Turin Foundation of Patrizia Sandretto Re Rebaudengo. Commenting on the choice of location, she has noted that 'I was interested in the life of a district different from the traditional touristic ones and the impact that artistic and cultural activities may have on the social fabric.' The new branch of the foundation plans to focus on Spanish and Latin American artists.

Art in the city is not limited to formal museums and foundations. From the trendy Chueca neighbourhood, home to a clutch of contemporary spaces showing international and new-wave Spanish artists, to the Museum of Public Art in the sedate Salamanca district, with its outdoor sculpture garden, a stroll around Madrid reveals a world of imaginative art shows.

Look Up

One of the most iconic of Madrid's early twentieth-century buildings, the much-photographed Metropolis Building at the junction of Calle de Alcalá and the Gran Vía, is surmounted by the winged figure of victory, Nike. But she is far from alone. Above the busy streets of central Madrid there is a silent army in waiting: gods and goddesses, mythical beasts, warriors and charioteers are perched atop the buildings, poised to fly at, charge and trample the enemies of the city.

The Metropolis Building was completed in 1911, as the headquarters of La Unión y el Fénix insurance company, built by the Spanish architect Luis Esteve to the design of the French architects Jules and Raymond Fevrier. It has only been 'The Metropolis Building' since 1972, when it was purchased by the Metrópolis Seguros company, which has overseen a magnificent restoration.

The Metropolis winged Nike, designed by Spanish architect Federico Coullaut-Valera Mendigutia, was not the original guardian sculpture. This was Ganymede and the Phoenix (linking to the name of the previous owners – La Unión y el Fénix) and this sculpture can now be seen crowning the modern tower block Mutua Madrileña on the Paseo de la Castellana, 33. Two 'cousins' of the Fénix sculpture can also be seen further up the Gran Vía. One adorns the dome of number 32, the Madrid-Paris building which dates from 1924. Originally housing one of Madrid's first department stores, SEPU (Sociedad Española de Precios Únicos – always a cut-rate store), the building is now the central Madrid branch of Primark. At number 68, there is another splendid Ganymede and Phoenix, with much

Metropolis building with figure of Nike.

Ganymede and the Phoenix
at Gran Vía, 32.

finer detailing, atop more former offices of La Unión y el Fénix, now an apartment building. In commissioning the sculptures, the company seems to have got its classical myths a little muddled. The phoenix, the legendary bird which dies in a burst of flames and then returns from its ashes, was a very appropriate emblem for what was at the time mostly a fire insurance company. However, to then replace the emblem, when the company merged with La Unión, by the joint figures does not quite work, as Ganymede was kidnapped by Zeus, in the form of an eagle not a phoenix, and a sexually exploitative kidnapping may not have been exactly the kind of union the company wanted to be associated with. No matter, the sculptures remain as part of the wonderful 'other life' of the Gran Vía.

Running through the centre of Madrid from Plaza de Cibeles to Plaza de España, the Gran Vía is one of the busiest streets for traffic and pedestrians. It is lined with majestic buildings from the early twentieth century, which were originally cinemas, hotels, restaurants and theatres. Many of the theatres and cinemas have gone,

to be replaced with shops. But the hotels have survived, with many
that were distinctly shabby at the end of the twentieth century now
restored and improved to become four- and five-star establishments.
The Gran Vía is one of the most vibrant shopping streets, with international and designer brands well represented, but these shops are
in every major Western city. For a truly unique experience the visitor needs to take a break from the shopping frenzy and look up
to see the idiosyncratic embellishments to these lovely buildings.
The architectural styles are diverse, ranging from Art Deco, French
and Viennese influences, to neo-Mudéjar, the late nineteenth to
early twentieth-century style of 'new Moorish' architecture which
is closely linked to Madrid, where it achieved some of its greatest
successes.

Typical of the high standard of restoration is Gran Vía, 31, a
lovely Art Deco building that is now the Hyatt Central Hotel. The
goddess-guardian of the hotel is Diana the Huntress, who stands
with her bow drawn on one of the hotel's turrets, two of her hunting dogs at her heels. In a wonderfully quirky touch, three more
dogs have been added, leaping out of the adjoining turret. While
the building was completed in 1930, the sculpture is a new work,
by the Spanish architect and sculptor Natividad Sánchez Fernández
(b. 1960), modelled by her daughter. The sculpture, at 5 metres (16
ft) high and weighing nearly 2 tonnes, was erected in 2017 as part of
the total refurbishment and redesign of the hotel and continues the
tradition of crowning the buildings of Madrid with powerful mythic
beings. The hotel's rooftop bar, the Jardín de Diana, is open from
late spring to autumn for drinks and food, with a great view over
this part of the city and the goddess's protection while you imbibe.

The other place where you can enjoy a gin and tonic overlooked
by a goddess is at the roof terrace bar of Círculo de Bellas Artes, Calle
de Alcalá, 42. This is where Minerva stands guard, in her helmet,
with spear and shield, a work by the sculptor Juan Luis Vassallo, who
was born in Cádiz in 1908 and died in Madrid in 1986. The Circulo
de Bellas Artes was founded in 1880 as a private institution to support the arts and it moved to its iconic building in 1926, designed
by the architect Antonio Palacios. The centre puts on exhibitions,

Statue of Diana and hounds on the Gran Vía.

talks and performances. It has a bookshop, theatre and also a lovely ground-floor café, with original Art Deco lamps and more original artworks and sculptures.

This part of Madrid has many rooftop sculptures, one of the most spectacular being the charioteers on what was the Banco Bilbao central Madrid office. This was built on an oddly shaped plot of land at Calle de Alcalá, 16, completed in 1923 to a design by Ricardo Bastida. There is still a small branch of the bank BBVA there, with the building also housing the Ministry of the Environment and Territorial Planning. The two squat towers each hold a huge 'quadriga', a four-horsed Roman chariot with charioteer astride. They are by the Basque sculptor Higinio Basterra, who executed the work between 1920 and 1923, choosing an image of strength and power to personify the Basque bank in Madrid. The chariots were originally cast in gilt bronze, which must have been an amazing sight in the sunlight. During the Spanish Civil War they were painted over in matt black paint to prevent them being used as sighting points by the besieging Nationalist army – and they have stayed black ever since. They still look very impressive.

One of the magnificent
four-horse chariots at
Calle de Alcalá, 16.

Chariots were a popular motif, with another business choosing
to show its namesake riding a chariot. In 1919 the insurance company
Seguros La Aurora bought the late nineteenth-century mansion at
Paseo de Recoletos, 4, designed by Augustín Ortiz de Villajos for
Ramón Pla Monje, a businessman and philanthropist who had made
his fortune in Cuba. Of course, one of the first things the company
wanted to do, to show they had arrived, was to install a statue of
Aurora atop the building's dome. Aurora, the goddess of the dawn, is
holding the flame that will bring the day's light, driving her chariot,
again a four-horse *quadriga*. The sculpture is by Juan Adsuara and
pre-dates the BBVA chariots by three years. The Seguros La Aurora
was also a Basque business from Bilbao, so again, a powerful image
was chosen to show its economic strength to the citizens of Madrid.

One of the most impressive sculptural groups adorns the Ministry of Agriculture, opposite the Atocha station on the Paseo de la Infanta Isabel. Dating from 1897, the huge building was designed by Ricardo Velázquez and is topped with three suitably enormous sculptures by Augustin Queral, comprising an angel and two winged horses, with attendant figures. It was originally made in Carrara marble but was so heavy the group had to be replaced by a bronze copy. The marble originals flew away, landing on the roundabouts at the Glorieta de Legazpi and the Glorieta de Cadiz, to the south of the city. Although the figures are holding farming implements and leaves – to symbolize the world of agriculture and crops – they look rather warlike, perhaps because they seem about to do battle with the two fearsome griffins on the roof of the Atocha railway station across the road. The station is from the same era, although completed five years before the Ministry, in 1892, having replaced an earlier station building destroyed by fire. The station was designed by Alberto de Palacio Elissagne, who collaborated with Gustave Eiffel and the engineer Henry Saint James, who designed the monumental arched wrought-iron roof where the griffins perch.

One group of characters denied their chance to 'reach for the sky' are the Gothic kings. This group of statues, representing five Visigoth kings and the fifteen rulers of the early Christian kingdoms during the Reconquista, were intended to decorate the balustrade of the Royal Palace but were deemed too heavy by the engineers. Instead, they remain on parade around the palace, in the central gardens of the Plaza de Oriente and in the Sabatini Gardens. Although they have weathered since their creation in the early 1750s, it is clear that they were designed to be viewed at an elevated distance, as they lack fine detail and finish.

One of the most extraordinary of Madrid's skyline sculptures is the 'Crashed Angel' or, to give the work its proper title, Accidente aéreo (Aerial Accident) by the artist Miguel Ángel Ruiz Beato, on the rooftop terrace of Calle de los Milaneses, 3, just off Calle Mayor. The upside-down bronze figure, with twisted wings and his head out of sight, crashed into the roof, is a great curiosity. It was commissioned in 2005 and the artist explained, in an interview in El País,

The 'Crashed Angel', Calle de los Milaneses, 3.

that he imagined an angel flying off 10,000 years ago. When he returned, floating on his back to look up to the sky, he didn't realize that a city had grown up in the meantime, where he used to fly over meadows, resulting in this accident.

Lifting your view beyond the street-level shops, hotels and offices provides a rich reward in Madrid's remarkable collection of sculptures. The nineteenth-century tradition of invoking powerful symbols to crown the headquarters of important organizations, government ministries, financial institutions and railway companies has continued into modern times, albeit with some subtle twists along the way.

Carmen Maura and Rossy de Palma in
Women on the Verge of a Nervous Breakdown (1988).

Man of La Mancha

In 1967 a seventeen-year-old seminary student left his home in Calzada de Calatrava, a village in Spain's bleak La Mancha region, to seek his fortune in Madrid. To support himself in the capital he sold bric-a-brac in El Rastro, Madrid's Sunday flea market, and worked part-time in the warehouse of Telefónica, Spain's telecoms company, while making Super-8 underground movies. Some fifteen years later, Pedro Almodóvar had established himself as the beacon of La Movida, Madrid's cultural explosion of the post-Franco years. If among Spain's great film directors, Luis Buñuel was the bourgeoisie's secular critic and Carlos Saura the symbolist poet of the Franco regime's twilight, Almodóvar came to embody the cultural bacchanal that followed Franco's death in 1975.

Madrid held a fascination for Almodóvar from a very young age. His first image of Madrid was conveyed to him by his mother. 'Like a fairy tale,' he recalls, 'she told me of when she went to Madrid as a little girl and walked along Calle de Alcalá, which can be compared to Madrid's Broadway. Madrid represented the place where films were shown first and the city where everybody did their own thing. A dream, basically.'

Visiting Malasaña, Chueca and Lavapiés, you still find the persistently hip neighbourhoods that boast some of the city's trendiest bars and clubs, and where the 1 to 6 a.m. culture remains alive, vibrant and a source of great annoyance to the neighbours. Partying to the wee hours was the single overriding, in-your-face feature of Madrid's counterculture. In the Spain of the 1980s, Madrid symbolized La Movida and La Movida was Almodóvar.

The Flower of My Secret (1996): Marisa Paredes and Juan Echanove in the Plaza Mayor.

Almodóvar's films portray Madrid as a nihilistic city, immersed in hedonism and black comedy, seasoned with homosexual eroticism and a sprinkling of violence – yet simultaneously a hopeful place, where people could breathe freely after having emerged from four decades of tyranny. Indeed, under Franco, Almodóvar risked imprisonment as a homosexual. Almodóvar's film repertoire is quintessentially a product of the frenetic mood that took hold of Madrid in the eighties.

The outrageous young mould-breaker from La Mancha quickly took Spanish cinema so far beyond the clichéd perception of staid Spanish society that the poster for his film *Law of Desire* (1987) – the tale of a love triangle between a gay film-maker, his transsexual sister and a murderously obsessive stalker – was banned in France. The film contains one of the steamiest sequences in Almodóvar's films, in which Carmen Maura – the leading lady of the muses known in Spain as 'Almodóvar's women' – plays a transsexual actress who stops in the street on a hot summer night and demands of a sanitation worker: 'Hose me down! Don't be shy!' That scene was shot against the grand portico of Centro Cultural Conde Duque, a hub of galleries and performance spaces in the former barracks of the Royal Guard.

Broken Embraces (2009): Lluís Homar, Blanca Portillo and Tamar Novas in Bar Chicote.

Watching Almodóvar's films is like taking a virtual-reality tour through Madrid. Several of the hundreds of locations on the screen have become iconic symbols of the director's universe. The three soulless tower blocks in which the main characters of *What Have I Done to Deserve This?* (1984) lived were a landscape familiar to Almodóvar, who drove a van every day along the M-30 motorway when he worked for Telefónica. The Telefónica building's tower at the top of the Gran Vía is seen from the flat of Pepa, played by Carmen Maura, who lived in fashionable Calle Montalbán in what is perhaps Almodóvar's most celebrated comedy, *Women on the Verge of a Nervous Breakdown* (1988).

Almodóvar's celluloid journey through the underground haunts of Madrid takes the viewer to places well hidden from tour buses. There are some very recognizable sequences, such as one sweeping the Plaza Mayor in *The Flower of My Secret* (1995) and in *Live Flesh* (1997) the night panorama over the eighteenth-century Puerta de Alcalá, which is the point of entry into Madrid's solidly middle-class Salamanca district.

Broken Embraces (2009) brings to life one of Madrid's most *castizo* hangouts, Chicote cocktail bar in the Gran Vía, almost under the shadow of the Telefónica tower. The interior shows that little has changed here since the days when its tables were graced by the presence of regulars like Frank Sinatra, Ernest Hemingway, Bette Davis and Ava Gardner – who seduced the illustrious bullfighter Luis Miguel Domingo over Chicote's gins and tonics.

The Segovia Viaduct, a traditional suicide spot which links the Royal Palace and the area of Vistillas, was a protagonist of one of Almodóvar's grimmest films, *Matador* (1986), where its relationship with death is taken to the extreme. In a later film, the provocative comedy *I'm So Excited* (2013), one of the characters is involved in an attempted suicide on the viaduct.

In *Labyrinth of Passion* (1982) Madrid becomes an explosive and cosmopolitan city, the nerve centre of Almodóvar's world. He draws parallels with New York, in the street corners of Madrid's Prosperidad working-class district, the stylish profile of the Azca office blocks and the shops and bars along Calle de la Princesa. Madrid, he says, is just as contradictory and varied, a thousand cities in one. The Madrid of this film is also the Rastro flea market, where as a street vendor the director was able to observe the contrasts of Madrid characters, from the middle-class passers-by on a Sunday morning to the obsessive collectors of antiques and art, and the eclectic gaggle of hawkers of curios and unadorned junk. You can observe a good deal of seductive looks and flirting in El Rastro's La Bobia café, unmissable for a flea market visitor and a legendary spot on the Madrid scene.

When Almodóvar reflects on his cinematographic career, it is clear that whatever he made of Madrid, Madrid made him: 'I grew up, enjoyed life, suffered, got fat and developed myself in Madrid. And I achieved many other things in the same rhythm as the city. My life and my films are linked to Madrid like the two sides of a coin.'

Special Shops

As Gertrude Stein famously remarked, 'Whoever said "money can't buy happiness" simply didn't know where to go shopping.' Madrid provides some unique opportunities for many happy hours of shopping.

There are many specialist shops in Madrid, and many of them are also 'special', in the sense of being unique and cherished remnants of a time when nearly all shops were specialist, run by people who were expert in their goods, acting as adviser and guide to the customer. It is a very different experience to shop in these traditional emporia; you have to know what you want before you go in – it's not just a question of language. When shopping in a modern department store, or chain-store, the shop floor is open with all the goods on display (with really valuable stock in glass cases). The customer goes in, looks around and has often picked up two or three things and is on the way to pay before a shop assistant intervenes. We still remember the shock of going into a little haberdashery store in Madrid, twenty years ago, and being confronted by a bare counter and the walls all around filled with closed drawers, up to the ceiling, the shop-keeper behind the counter ready to serve us, if only we knew what we wanted.

The streets around Plaza Mayor are home to a host of haberdashery shops selling buttons, ribbons, trimmings and myriad specialist handicraft supplies, such as the bases for 'fascinator' hats, handles for cloth bags, shoulder pads and glass eyes for soft toys. And they are busy – the interest in crafts and needlework in all forms continues and is bolstered by these shops also offering courses in various arts and crafts. Some of the specialist shops are almost absurdly so, such as the Fieltros Olleros, just south of the Plaza Mayor on Plaza Comandante Las Morenas, which sells only felt. The bales of intensely coloured, soft fabric look so inviting that we have been desperate to buy some but, despite racking our brains for about ten minutes, we really couldn't think of any reasonable use for yards of felt.

We have had more purchasing opportunities at the confectioner La Violeta, in Plaza de Canalejas, 6, near the Sevilla metro station, which sells sugar-crystallized real violets and violet-flavoured, flower-shaped boiled sweets. They have recently branched out and now sell violet-petal-infused tea and raspberry and blackberry sweets, but it's really all about the violets. La Violeta is a tiny bijoux shop with an original 1915 wooden facade and curved glass windows. Inside it's a purple haze of cabinets and shelves, full of different-sized containers of the violet sweets, going up in degrees of fanciness and fancifulness. Famous customers of the past include Jacinto Benavente, the Nobel Prize-winning playwright, and Queen Victoria Eugenie, wife of Alfonso XIII. The shop is still a family business, now run by María and Mónica, granddaughters of the founder, Mariano Gil Fernández. The sweets are delightful, with a hard but then chewy texture and a strong violet taste, which means that you only ever want to eat a few at a time. We now restrict ourselves to buying the sweets in the purple cardboard packs, as we already have so many violet-adorned tins, bonbon dishes, porcelain boxes and the like, all of which arrived crammed with *violeta* sweets.

Some shops specialize in a particular delicacy or two, made on the premises. For example, the churrería Hermanos Fernanz, in Calle de Castelló, Barrio de Salamanca, sells two things; churros and kettle chips – not just made on the premises but in front of your eyes: in seconds a hopper of potatoes are sliced, dropping through to the boiling oil and in two turns of the giant scoop a huge tray of crisps are fried to golden perfection. A wonderful confectionery-buying experience is at Casa Mira, on Calle de San Jerónimo. Here the giant slabs of *turrón* – nougat confectionary with toasted almonds or other nuts – are cut to your requirement, wrapped in waxed paper and

The purple haze of La Violeta.

tied with parcel ribbon. It has the delightfully old-fashioned system whereby the assistant gives you a handwritten invoice to take to the cash desk, across the shop; when you have had your invoice stamped as 'paid', you can then return to pick up your *turrón* from the counter. The disadvantage is that because the best *turrón* is made from expensive almonds, candied fruit and fine chocolate it is very heavy and choosing a bit of this one and then that one, because they all looked so delicious, plus some glacé apricots and pineapple slices, we can find we have spent €60 on some sweet 'extras' for Christmas. Still, it is the finest you can get.

A more unusual place to buy confectionery is the Corpus Christi convent, in Plaza del Conde de Miranda, just behind the Mercado de San Miguel. The convent is also known as the Convento de las Carboneras (Convent of the Coal Merchants), owing to the legend that a picture of the Immaculate Conception was found in a coal cellar and presented to the nuns. The convent was founded in the reign of Felipe III and is housed in the original buildings, designed by the architect Miguel de Soria. The nuns here make eight different sorts of sweets, pastries and biscuits, available in kilogram or half-kilogram packages. Varieties include *rosquillas* (slightly aniseed-flavoured rings of crunchy dough), almond biscuits, tea biscuits, *naranjines* (dark chocolate and orange sweets), *mantecados* (basically lard and sugar; sounds awful, but they are a delicious, calorific bomb) and *polverones*, so crumbly you have to squash the little cake together before you try to unwrap it.

Buying the biscuits was a trip into a different, quiet world. It started with finding the right door to the convent – the tiled arrow

Confectionery at Casa Mira.

indicating 'No. 3' helped – then spotting beside a huge door, a small door, with an intercom sporting a notice giving the hours for sales of sweets. After buzzing the intercom, we waited, and waited, buzzed again and were about to give up, when in response to a feeble buzz we were able to open the door. This opened onto a hallway but no sign of a pastry shop, so we carried on and came to a sign pointing to 'Torno'. We crossed a courtyard and into another hallway where a wooden shuttered window opened on the hatch where the pastries are sold. Because the nuns are cloistered, the *torno*, a cross between a wooden revolving door and a 'lazy susan', enables them to make the transactions without seeing, or being in the same room, as their customers. Beside the hatch there's a price list for the biscuits. We rang another bell and waited for a nun. After another couple of minutes, we heard footsteps and then '¿Sí?' We gave our order, the *torno* turned and there were the biscuits. We put a €20 note in their place and turned the *torno*, another turn and there was the change. We retraced our steps with a sense of achievement.

Another special shop that slightly takes one back in time is 'Capas Seseña', makers of capes, and only capes, albeit a mix of traditional and more modern designs. The business was started in 1901 by Santos Seseña, and is now run by his great-grandson Marcos, who, working with a small, skilled team, makes the capes on the premises. Beyond the showroom you can see the fabric laid out, with huge cutting-out scissors, dark fabric for the flowing outer layer and flashes of brilliant blue and scarlet lining material. The list of aristocrats, celebrities and artist customers is endless, with many tales of intense attachment to their Capas Seseña capes. Orson Welles famously wore his cape to advertise sherry from the Domecq winery, Picasso left instructions to be buried in his and more recent customers include Plácido Domingo and Nicolas Cage.

Capas Seseña's iconic style is still the gentleman's '1901' model. However, in 1960 they took the bold step of also producing a range of women's capes, with several classic designs and fashion numbers which change season by season. Try on a cape and the impulse to twirl around is irresistible, swishing the fabric and experimenting with it flung back over the shoulders or wrapped around and cosily

Tailoring a cape at Capas Seseña.

'muffled' at the neck. Marcos and his staff offer expert instruction on how to manage the yards of fabric elegantly (there is also a YouTube video produced by the shop, 'Instructions for the use of a Spanish cape'!). Capes are a long-established part of the Spanish 'look', despite the attempt to ban them in 1766 by Carlos III's Italian-born minister, the Marquis of Esquilache, due to the fear that the long cape could be used as a disguise or to conceal weapons.

Fashion-forward Madrid is a marvellous place to buy original, stylish shoes in the softest of leathers and a mix of traditional and quirky designs, made in Spain and in some cases in the workshop behind the shop. The streets around the Plaza Mayor include several old-time *Cordelerías* making the traditional canvas upper and rope-soled espadrilles in a range of rainbow hues. These have now been joined by more modern designer shops, taking the humble espa-drille to new heights (literally, in the case of wedge heels) with all manner of stylistic additions, including ankle straps, sling backs, embroidered and embellished uppers, laces and a wide range of leather and suede models in addition to the original canvas styles.

For more formal shoes, the high society ladies of Madrid make their way to 'Franjul' in the Barrio de las Letras. Here, shoes are custom-made to order, in the style, colour, heel height and finish to match your designer outfit. Our latest, favourite shoe shop is the quirkily named De Flores y Floreros (Of Flowers and Flowerpots) on Calle del Almirante, with its highly original, jewel-bright shoes in a range of flat to medium-heeled styles, including lace-ups, tasselled loafers, Mary-Janes and ballerina pumps. Not only do they look adorable, they are supremely comfortable to wear.

The ultimate special shop in Madrid must be the Royal Tapestry Factory, founded in 1721 by Felipe v, which although not on its original site, has been in the current premises on the Calle de Fuenterrabía for over a century, since 1889. The tapestry factory presents a fascinating window into a large-scale craft enterprise of the sort that exists almost nowhere else today. For anyone with an interest in textiles and weaving it is a must, with guided tours daily and, unlike a museum, you can actually order your own tapestry, as these are still made to the original Goya cartoons. The artist produced these for the factory between 1775 and 1791, with tapestries commissioned by both Carlos III and Carlos IV to hang in the San Lorenzo de El

The Royal Tapestry workshop.

Escorial and El Pardo palaces. Goya was at that time a young and little-known artist, so although not a prestigious commission in themselves, the tapestry designs were a chance to bring himself to wider attention. The Royal Tapestry Factory also still produces handmade carpets to bespoke heraldic designs, or copies to replace historic pieces. These are made to order for the royal palaces of Spain and the country's cathedrals.

LISTINGS

Sights

Puerta del Sol
Metro: Sol
The Puerta del Sol is very much at the heart of historic Madrid and any visitor is bound to pass through it a number of times, going from the Royal Palace to the Retiro Park, for example, or the Plaza Mayor to the Gran Vía. The Puerta del Sol was the eastern gate to the early city and later became the main gathering point to hear the city news. It is still a major meeting place and is the traditional place to hear the New Year's Eve chimes from the clock tower on the main building on the south side, now the administrative centre for the Madrid autonomous region. Other sights in the square are the Bear and the Strawberry tree statue, a symbol of Madrid; a statue of Carlos III, the 'king-mayor' who initiated many of the current city landmarks in the eighteenth century; and the famous illuminated Tío Pepe sign on the northern side of the square.

Parque del Buen Retiro
Metro: Retiro (north side); Atocha de Renfe (south side)
The Retiro Park offers a peaceful haven away from the crowded Madrid streets. It has been a public park since the late eighteenth century, having previously been a royal retreat. The park is composed of semi-formal gardens, with gravel walkways and much statuary. There are several playgrounds for children, an area with outdoor gym equipment for adults and the Estanque, a large artificial boating lake, with rowing boats for hire, overlooked by an equestrian statue of Alfonso XII. The park has three small art galleries housed in historic buildings, the Casa de Vacas, the Palacio de Velázquez and the Palacio de Cristal, which hold temporary exhibitions, usually of modern and contemporary art.

Plaza Mayor
Metro: Sol
The Plaza Mayor is, as the name suggests, large, and the vast cobbled square can feel surprisingly empty unless there is a seasonal event going on. A famous statue of Felipe III dominates the square and surrounding

attractive buildings, whose uniformity is broken by the twin-turreted Casa de la Panadería, once the central office for regulating sales of bread. The edges of the square are full of café tables and it is a great spot to stop for a drink and a snack while sightseeing. The square also hosts caricature artists, street performers and 'living statues'. At Christmas time, the square is filled with stalls selling the figures for *belenes*, the nativity scenes that are the traditional Christmas decoration in Spanish homes.

Palacio Real

Calle de Bailén, 28071 Madrid
Metro: Ópera
The vast Royal Palace, with more than 3,000 rooms – the most in Europe – is on the site of the old Alcázar palace, which burnt down at Christmas in 1734. The new palace took over thirty years to complete and Carlos III was the first monarch to reside there. The royal family no longer live in the palace, but it is used for state occasions. The opulently decorated state rooms are open to the public, hung with paintings by Velázquez, Goya, Caravaggio and a host of other Old Masters, adorned with gilded mirrors and massive chandeliers, with antique furniture and porcelain also on display. It also has the only string quintet in the world in which every instrument was made by Stradivarius. The palace houses the royal armoury, including armour for the knights' horses.

Barrio de las Letras

Metro: Sevilla, Antón Martín
A warren of small streets bounded by Carrera de San Jerónimo to the north, Calle de Atocha to the south, and between Calle de la Cruz to the west and Paseo del Prado to the east.

A lovely area to stroll around, the Barrio de las Letras celebrates the Golden Age of Spanish literature when Lope de Vega, Cervantes, Góngora and Quevedo all lived in these streets. The area is full of bars and cafés, independent boutiques and antique shops. Lope de Vega's house has been wonderfully restored. It is furnished with furniture and objects of the period that have been assembled following an inventory of his possessions from 1627, so the house gives a very authentic feel for how the playwright lived. Also restored is the charming garden of which he wrote 'My garden, smaller than a kite, has only two trees, ten flowers, two vines, a white musk rose.'

El Real Jardín Botánico

Paseo del Prado, 28014 Madrid
Metro: Atocha
If you need a rest from viewing art, the Jardín Botánico is located just beyond the Prado Museum, walking towards the Atocha station. It provides a quiet place for a relaxing stroll through 9 hectares (22 ac.) of beautifully planted formal gardens, with more than 30,000 species represented.

Madrid Río Park

Puente de Toledo, 28019 Madrid
Metro: Pirámides
The park was created to renovate the post-industrial riverside and has resulted in a wonderful new space to escape from the city streets for a stroll by the river. The park extends over more than 6 kilometres (4 mi.) and it is possible to hire bikes. There are seventeen different play spots for children, including slides built into the rock, climbing frames and zip wires, plus a huge fountain to run through in the summer. The Arguenzuela footbridge is a highlight of modern design, covered in silver mesh, while the Baroque Puente de Toledo, with its statue of San Isidro, is now a highlight of the modern park.

Ermita de San Antonio de la Florida

Glorieta de San Antonio de la Florida, 5, 28008 Madrid
Metro: Principe Pío
A small chapel decorated with beautiful frescoes by Goya, which make powerful use of light and perspective to portray vivid scenes of the miracles of St Anthony, with angels and townsfolk looking on. The chapel has also been the site of Goya's tomb since his remains were transferred here in 1919.

Almudena Cathedral

Calle de Bailén, 10, 28013 Madrid

Metro: Ópera

Madrid's long-delayed cathedral. Plans to build a cathedral for the capital started to be discussed in the sixteenth century, but no design was agreed until 1879 and work on the building finally started in 1883. Due to political turmoil and financial constraints it was only completed and consecrated in 1993. The Almudena is Neo-Gothic in style, with a light and airy interior.

Atocha Railway Station

Calle Atocha

Metro: Atocha; Atocha Renfe

Yes really, do go to the station, even if you're not catching a train. The nineteenth-century buildings have been beautifully restored and include an indoor palm plantation and terrapin pool, as well as several bars and cafés. The impressive exterior of the station features a large clock, together with carved griffins on the roof.

Museums

The 'Golden Triangle' of the three major galleries – the Prado, Reina Sofía and the Museo Thyssen-Bornemisza – makes Madrid a major destination for devotees of fine art. It is worth buying the 'Abono Paseo del Arte' ticket, which grants entry to each of the three museums once within a year of purchase.

Museo del Prado

Edificio Villanueva, Paseo del Prado, 28014 Madrid

Metro: Atocha; Banco De España; Sevilla; or Antón Martin

The Prado is the original art gallery – the 'big one', responsible on its own for drawing in many thousands of Madrid's tourists. As with all blockbuster attractions, there's a reason for this, it simply has one of the highest concentrations of Old Masters of any gallery in the world. Highlights are the Velázquez, Goya and El Greco collections.

Museo National Centro de Arte Reina Sofía

Calle de Santa Isabel, 32, 28012 Madrid

Metro: Atocha

Established in 1992, the museum houses the national collection of twentieth-century modern art. The building's monumental proportions and austere style create the perfect space for large pieces, in particular its star attraction, *Guernica*, Picasso's testament to the bombing of civilians in the Basque town during the Civil War.

Museo Thyssen-Bornemisza

Paso del Prado, 8, 28015, Madrid

Metro: Banco de España

A smaller and more manageable collection to view, showcasing wonderful examples of Western art through the ages, with especially good selections from nineteenth- and early twentieth-century art movements. It has an excellent bookshop and design-orientated gift shop.

Smaller Galleries and Museums

Centro Conde Duque Contemporary Art Museum

Calle Conde Duque, 11, 28015 Madrid

Metro: Ventura Rodríguez

Spacious arts centre in the old barracks building. The contemporary art collection is on the first and second floors, featuring current Spanish artists and a chronological layout starting from around 1920. The final section is an evolving 'new creators' display.

Caixa Forum

Paseo del Prado, 36, 28014 Madrid

Metro: Atocha

The main exhibition space of the Catalan bank's foundation in Madrid, which runs a programme of temporary exhibitions of fine art, photography, design and, occasionally, archaeology.

Espacio Fundación Telefónica
Calle de Fuencarral, 3, 28004 Madrid
Metro: Gran Vía
Permanent exhibition tracing the history of telecommunications, in particular developments in technology and their impact in Spain. On other floors, there are temporary exhibitions with an emphasis on photography, film and the boundaries of art and technology. The Fundación puts on some unusual and thought-provoking shows.

Fundación MAPFRE
Paseo de Recoletos, 23 and Calle de Bárbara Braganza, 13, 28004 Madrid
Metro: Colón
The Fundación has two exhibition spaces just around the corner from each other. Sala Recoletos has a permanent Miró exhibition, plus a wide-ranging programme of temporary art exhibitions, while Sala Bárbara de Braganza focuses on photography exhibitions.

Matadero Art Centre
Paseo de la Chopera 14, 28045 Madrid
Metro: Legazpi
Housed in the converted main cattle market and slaughterhouse, this huge complex includes exhibits of contemporary art and design, workshop spaces, a lecture auditorium, theatre space, installations and a vast outdoor area for craft markets, festival performances and much more.

Museo del Romanticismo
Calle de San Mateo, 13, 28004 Madrid
Metro: Tribunal
An absolute gem of a museum in an eighteenth-century Neoclassical palace. The museum was established in this building in 1924, by the Marquis de Vega-Inclán, a collector of works from the artistic and literary movement of Romanticism, which reached its height in the nineteenth century. The rooms are beautifully laid out with paintings, furniture and decorative arts, aiming to capture the atmosphere of

Spanish Romanticism and portray aspects of the society that gave rise to it. It also has a great shop with a good selection of books and high-quality gifts such as jewellery, fans and scarves.

Museo National de Artes Decorativas

Calle Montalbán, 12, 28014 Madrid
Metro: Banco de España or Retiro
The star of the Museo National de Artes Decorativas is the eighteenth-century tiled kitchen from Valencia, featuring illustrations of food and kitchen scenes, including a cat tugging at a large fish. Over the museum's five floors there are other detailed room displays that show off the furniture and furnishings across the centuries, and wonderful collections of fans and Talavera ceramics. The museum also has temporary exhibitions of contemporary crafts, such as jewellery and ceramics. The great frustration is that there is no museum shop.

Royal Tapestry Factory

Calle Fuenterrabía, 2, 28014 Madrid
Metro: Atocha Renfe
Strictly speaking, this is not a museum but an active workshop, still producing handmade tapestries and carpets for clientele from royal palaces and cathedrals to the Ritz Hotel. Daily tours Monday to Friday offer the opportunity to see the workshop's collection of historic tapestries and to observe weaving in progress by the skilled workforce, some using looms that have been in constant use since the workshop moved to its current premises in 1889.

Museo Sorralla

Paseo del General Martínez Campos, 28010 Madrid
Metro: Gregorio Marañon
Charming studio-museum, with the largest collection of works by Joaquín Sorolla, housed in the building where the artist lived and worked, which his widow donated to the state. Sorolla's reputation and popularity have revived in the past fifty years, as his paintings are appreciated for their freshness and luminous portrayals of sunshine and sea. The studio rooms have been left almost as they were in the artist's

day, with eclectic objects from his travels around Spain. The surrounding Andalucian-style gardens are a cool delight.

Museo Cerralbo

Calle Ventura Rodríguez, 17, 28008 Madrid
Metro: Plaza de España
Housed in the nineteenth-century, neo-Baroque palace of the Marquis of Cerralbo, the museum shows the marquis' collection of paintings, antique furniture, decorative objects and an array of historic weapons. There are more than 50,000 objects in total, almost exactly as they were left when bequeathed to the Spanish state in 1922. To preserve the feel of the aristocratic household, the exhibits are piled up on tables and in display cabinets, with very little information signposted, so it can feel a bit overwhelming. Nonetheless, definitely worth a look.

Museo del Traje

Avenida de Juan de Herrera, 2, 28040 Madrid
Metro: Moncloa
Focusing on the evolution of Spanish design and fashion, the museum is relatively new, having opened in 2004 in a modern building to the north of the city, off the usual tourist routes. It has a wonderful collection of eighteenth-century court dress and regional costumes from around Spain, as well as an extensive fashion collection by twentieth-century and contemporary Spanish designers. It also operates an ongoing programme of temporary exhibitions focused on particular periods and designers. The museum has a good design-led shop for books and accessories.

Hotels

The number of hotels in Madrid has increased dramatically in recent years to cope with the tourist boom, catering to all levels of the market. The city is awash with four- and five-star hotels and there are several reliable mid-priced hotel chains with sites in central locations. We suggest a few independent hotels, from super-luxe to comfortable hostels that have a special 'Madrid' feel to them.

Gran Hotel Inglés

Calle de Echegaray, 8, 28014 Madrid

Metro: Sevilla

What was a modest *pensión* in this central historic street has had a major refurbishment to emerge as an exclusive deluxe hotel, with an individual touch. Right in the centre of Madrid, with easy walking access to main sights, great bars and restaurants.

Hotel Único

Calle de Claudio Coello, 67, 28001 Madrid

Metro: Serrano

A boutique hotel in a restored nineteenth-century mansion, with modern décor and amenities. It is situated in the heart of the fashion district, in Calle de Claudio Coello, famous for its exclusive boutiques and Spanish design stores. It is also very central for museums and galleries.

Hotel Wellington

Calle de Velázquez, 8, 28001 Madrid

Metro: Retiro

The Wellington is an established luxury hotel in the Salamanca district, furnished in a comfortably grand style. It has long been known as Madrid's 'bullfighters' hotel', and is still a favourite with the matadors and their entourages. The hotel has an outdoor swimming pool and is just five minutes' walk from Retiro Park.

URSO Hotel and Spa

Calle de Mejía Lequerica 8, 28004 Madrid

Metro: Bilbao, Alonso Martínez

Boutique hotel, close to main tourist attractions, with well-furnished rooms and located in an area that is quiet at night. Has the added benefit of a spa to aid relaxation after a day of sightseeing and gallery-visiting. Guests also rave about the breakfast buffet.

Only YOU Hotel
Calle del Barquillo 21, 28004 Madrid
Metro: Chueca
Stylish boutique hotel in the trendy Chueca district, glorious
over-the-top interiors with comfortable rooms, attentive staff
and a gluten-free bakery and café. In a great area for nightlife
and close to major sights.

Posada del León de Oro
Cava Baja 12, 28005 Madrid
Metro: La Latina
A small hotel above an old tavern in the centre of historic Madrid,
it still has a public bar and restaurant on the ground floor. The rooms
are on the small side but full of character, with individual decoration
and Wi-Fi throughout. Staff are friendly and helpful, and the posada
is good value for its central location.

Escala Ópera Guest House
Calle de Arrieta 2, 2a Planta, 28013 Madrid
Metro: Ópera
A hidden gem on the second floor of a two-hundred-year-old historic
building in the Ópera district. The rooms are furnished with antiques,
creating a unique atmosphere, while it also has modern amenities,
comfortable beds and Wi-Fi. Balcony rooms offer the chance to look
out over the Plaza de Oriente.

Hostal Alexis Madrid
Calle del Príncipe, 18, Piso 4, 28012 Madrid
Metro: Sevilla
A small *pensión* on the fourth floor of a nineteenth-century building in
the very central Calle del Príncipe, close to the major historic sights and
a great area for bars and restaurants. Although it is close to the nightlife,
the accommodation is quiet. The rooms are comfortable and clean, with
air conditioning and Wi-Fi.

Entertainment Venues

Teatro Real – Opera
Plaza de Isabel II, 28013 Madrid
Metro: Ópera
www.teatroreal.es/en
El Teatro Real, situated just in front of the Royal Palace, first opened in 1850 as one of Europe's grandest venues. After 75 years of performances, it closed in 1925 due to subsidence of the building and remained closed for 41 years. After extensive repairs it was used as a concert hall from 1966 to 1988, when it was decided to restore the building as an opera house. It is now established as the premier venue for opera and ballet in Madrid, with world-class singers and international ballet companies visiting. It also shows flamenco and concerts. Shows tend to sell out, so it is best to book in advance through the website. It is also possible to take a tour of the opera house, available most days between 10.30 a.m. and 4.30 p.m.

Corral de la Morería - Flamenco
Calle de la Morería, 17, 28005 Madrid
Metro: La Latina
www.corraldelamoreria.com
This is one of the most established flamenco *tablaos* in Madrid. It is quite expensive and a bit touristy but they get some of the finest dancers and musicians performing, so it is flamenco from the heart, not just a floor show that's all about the dresses and some kicks. Open Monday to Sunday, the venue has the option to book a show with dinner, or with just a drink.

Casa Patas – Flamenco
Calle de Cañizares, 10, 28012 Madrid
Metro: Tirso de Molino
http://casapatas.com/casa-patas-2/
Another well-established and highly recommended venue for flamenco dancing, with nightly shows from Monday to Saturday. There are also special performances by top flamenco singers and guitarists in the Sala García Lorca upstairs.

Teatro de la Comedia – National Classical Theatre Company

Calle Príncipe, 14, 28012 Madrid

Metro: Sevilla

http://teatroclasico.mcu.es

This wonderful old theatre, appropriately situated in the heart of the Barrio de las Letras, is the home of the Compañia National de Teatro Clasico, dedicated to performing the works of the Golden Age dramatists: Lope De Vega, Calderón de la Barca, Miguel de Cervantes and Tirso de Molina, as well as later classics by authors such as Jacinto Benavente. The theatre has a spectacular interior, which underwent restoration between 2012 and 2015.

Teatro de la Zarzuela

Calle de Jovellanos 4, 28014 Madrid

Metro: Sevilla

http://teatrodelazarzuela.mcu.es/en/

Zarzuela is the traditional comic-opera style of Madrid. It emerged in the seventeenth century and is a cross between a play and a musical, usually with a lot of humour as well. The best-known zarzuela composers include Francisco Asenjo Barbieri, Federico de Chueca, Ruperto Chapí and Joaquín Gaztambide. Many of the classic musicals feature streetwise Madrid types as characters and they are often set in the most traditional areas of the city. The Teatro de la Zarzuela is the only theatre dedicated to Spanish light opera. It first opened in 1856, modelled on La Scala in Milan and after many transformations and re-modelling was declared a national monument in 1994. In addition to the zarzuela operas, dance performances, plays and concerts are also presented.

Café Central – Jazz

Plaza del Ángel, 10, 28012 Madrid

Metro: Tirso de Molina

www.cafecentralmadrid.com/en/

Traditional café off Plaza de Santa Ana with live jazz or blues most nights from about 10 p.m. Popular with locals and tourists, it attracts a crowd of all ages and nationalities. Often quite packed, but with a very friendly atmosphere.

Sala Clamores – Jazz and Soul

Calle de Alburquerque, 14, 28010 Madrid

Metro: Bilbao

www.salaclamores.es

A basement club in the Chamberí district, hosting musicians from all over the world. Featuring mainly jazz and soul artists, there are also folk, tango and blues nights. The marble tables are packed in, so once you have secured your seat you are in for the night, but the waiting staff have great skills at getting through with beers and cocktails.

Auditoria Nacional de Música

Calle del Príncipe de Vergara, 146, 28002 Madrid

Metro: Cruz del Rayo

www.auditorionacional.mcu.es/en/

The main classical music venue in Madrid, the national auditorium has two halls: a symphony hall and a smaller chamber music venue. It is home to the Spanish National Orchestra and Youth Orchestra. The Madrid Festival Orchestra and the Real Conservatorio Superior de Música de Madrid also regularly perform here.

Bernabéu Stadium – Home of Real Madrid Football Team

Av. de Concha Espina, 1, 28036 Madrid

Metro: Santiago Bernabéu

www.realmadrid.com/en/santiago-bernabeu-stadium

A must for all football fans, and even those who aren't followers of the beautiful game admit that it is a magnificent stadium. The tour is comprehensive, with access to a lot of areas (on non-match days) and of course an impressive array of silverware. The atmosphere at a game is great – noisy but not aggressive. It is possible to buy tickets for regular league matches online. Daily tours of the stadium are available on non-match days from 10.30 a.m. to 6.30 p.m. and on match days up to five hours before kick-off.

Sala La Riviera

Paseo Bajo de la Vírgen del Puerto, 28005 Madrid
Metro: Príncipe Pio; Puerta del Ángel
Landmark live music venue right by the Manzanares River, near the
Puente de Segovia. It has a large auditorium for live gigs, and on club
nights a huge circular dance floor which opens out on to a terrace,
making it a favourite venue for summer nights, as a breeze from the
river can cool it down by a few degrees. La Riviera puts on live shows
by some of the biggest names in Spanish pop, as well as up-and-coming
bands. Live music events usually start around 8 p.m., while the night
club at weekends is from midnight to 6 a.m.

Restaurants

The restaurants listed are all Spanish style, with some of the most
castizo of Madrid food, together with some specializing in other
regional Spanish styles. However, there is also a myriad of exotic
cuisines in Madrid. The city has long had excellent Japanese restaurants,
now joined by some very good Chinese, Thai and other Asian and South
American eateries. It is advisable to book a table in advance for lunch
or dinner.

La Huerta de Tudela

Calle del Prado, 15, 28014 Madrid
+91 4204418
Metro: Sevilla
A great place for vegetable dishes – although several have additions
such as serrano ham or prawns, so vegetarians need to check the
ingredients. Much of the produce comes from Tudela, the vegetable
garden of Spain. The restaurant does a range of tasting menus, a good
opportunity to sample the wide range of amazing things they can do
with celery, onions, potatoes, peppers and beans.

Casa Macareno
Calle de San Vicente Ferrer, 44, 28004 Madrid
+ 91 1660921
Metro: Tribunal
This bar and restaurant lies in the heart of the cool neighbourhood
of Malasaña. It combines the best of the traditional with its tiled décor
and menu of tapas staples, such as *croquetas*, 'broken eggs' and *patatas
bravas*, with a modern emphasis on high-quality ingredients and the
introduction of some gourmet dishes, including sea bream *tiradito* and
cod gratin. The bar gets very busy, as does the small restaurant,
so booking is essential if you want to secure a table for dinner.

La Bien Aparecida
Calle de Jorge Juan, 8, 28001 Madrid
+ 91 1593939
Metro: Serrano; Príncipe de Vergara
Fine dining in the heart of the fashion district. Appropriately, the
chef gives an up-to-date twist to Spanish and European dishes,
such as amuse-bouches of miniature *bocadillos* of steak tartare,
light and fluffy *croquetas de jamón* and a 'lasagna' of layered red
peppers and anchovies.

Bars and Cafés

There are many different types of establishments in which to eat
and drink in Madrid, from cool, modern coffee shops, to traditional
cafés, to bars – each with its own distinctive character. While most
of these also serve meals, it's a different experience from eating in
a restaurant. The newest places for a late-night drink are the rooftop
terraces, where an exquisite gin and tonic comes with a marvellous
view of the city.

Cervecería Alemana

Plaza de Santa Ana, 6, 28012 Madrid
Metro: Sol
The most traditional of the many bars and cafés in this central square, with a good selection of *pinchos* and *raciones,* plus the table where Ernest Hemingway used to sit.

El Brillante

Plaza Emperador Carlos v, 8, 28012 Madrid
Metro: Atocha
No-nonsense, large, bright and noisy café bar, close to the Reina Sofía Museum and Atocha station. The *bocadillo de calamares* is indeed the stuff of legends, and the staff include some of most *castizo* waiters in Madrid. Great for breakfast, or a post-museum snack, open 6.30 a.m. to midnight.

La Venencia

Calle Echegaray, 7, 28014 Madrid
Metro: Sevilla
Old-fashioned sherry bar that's quite unique in Madrid. It is named after the long narrow ladle that is used to sample sherry from the cask. Note it only serves sherry – a range of styles, including fino, manzanilla, oloroso – but no other drinks. There are small snacks to accompany the sherry, of olives, nuts, cheese or charcuterie. House rules are no photography and no tips.

Casa Maravillas

Calle de Jorge Juan, 54 (corner of Calle Príncipe de Vergara) 28001 Madrid
Metro: Principe de Vergara
Busy neighbourhood bar in a traditional style with good seafood *raciones*. The small restaurant prides itself on serving traditional Madrid dishes such as *cocido* (chickpea stew) and *callos* (tripe), as well as market-fresh fish of the day.

La Colmada

Calle del Espíritu Santo, 19, 28004 Madrid

Metro: Tribunal

Bright café and delicatessen in the trendy Malasaña district, it has a great range of charcuterie and vermouth to drink in or buy from the bottle store and take home.

Casa González

Calle del León, 12, 28014 Madrid

Metro: Antón Martín

Charming bar and delicatessen shop in the Barrio de las Letras, a great place to pop into for a coffee, light lunch or evening glass of wine with tapas. It has one of the best selections of cheese, plus Ibérico meats, olive oils and preserves. The bar is always very busy at weekends as it is a favourite spot among the locals as well as visitors.

El Madroño

Plaza Puerta Cerrada, 7, 28005 Madrid

Metro: La Latina

Over a hundred years old, with a lovely tiled interior, the bar is named after the *madroño*, the strawberry tree symbol of Madrid. It is famous for the sweet liqueur made from the *madroño* berries, served in little chocolate-lined wafer cups – well worth trying (although you probably wouldn't want to drink it all night). The bar also serves the usual range of drinks, together with traditional Spanish fare in the restaurant.

Bar Cock

Calle de la Reina, 16, 28004 Madrid

Metro: Gran Vía

A tucked-away cocktail bar that is not as loud and glitzy as most, so you can enjoy a well-crafted, traditional cocktail in the softly lit and usually quiet interior. It's a great place to end a night out with a very civilized drink after dinner.

Círculo de Bellas Artes – Terraza

Calle de Acalá, 42, 28014 Madrid

Metro: Sevilla

The rooftop terrace of the Café del Círculo de Bellas Artes is open in the summer months. It charges a small entry fee but is worth it for the superb views of central Madrid and the relaxed vibe, with loungers and artificial grass, plus a full range of cocktails, wine and beers. It is also great for a good view with a drink and snack during the day. The ground floor café is a wonderful Art Deco-style space with sculptures and painted ceiling, serving drinks, tapas and a full lunch/dinner menu.

Terraza Cibeles

Palacio de Cibeles, Plaza de Cibeles, 1, 28014 Madrid

Metro: Banco de España

Rooftop terrace for gin and tonic, cocktails and other drinks. Again, there is a small entry fee, but great views over the Cibeles statue, down the Paseo de Prado and up to the Puerta de Alcalá.

Café Gijón

Paseo de Recoletos, 21, 28004 Madrid

Metro: Banco de España

One of the remaining iconic cafés that has been a favourite with writers and artists since the nineteenth century. Café Gijón also has a spacious terrace bar in the Paseo de Recoletos in the summer months. The café is open from morning until late at night for coffee, drinks and *raciones*, as well as lunch and dinner. It has a good deal for the *menú del día* at lunchtime.

Café Comercial

Glorieta de Bilbao, 7, 28004 Madrid

Metro: Bilbao

Classic old-style Madrid café now refurbished to its former glory. It has three distinct spaces: the bar, the café and a beautifully refurbished restaurant upstairs. Definitely a place to linger with coffee or a drink, reading the papers, or people-watching – your choice! Open 8 a.m. to 1 a.m.

Café de la Luz

Calle de Puebla, 8, 28004 Madrid

Metro: Gran Vía

Cosy kitsch interior, with vintage décor and couches, a place where you can start to feel very at home with a coffee, or a cocktail later in the day. Food menu includes breakfast, toasted sandwiches and cakes, so somewhere for a drink and a snack rather than a full meal. Open 8 a.m. to 2 a.m.

Café del Nuncio

Calle de Segovia 9, 28005 Madrid

Metro: La Latina

Established in 1877, this café has recently undergone a complete modernization by the Café Angélica coffee-roasting company, which has brought a lighter, brighter interior and better coffee but has done away with the nostalgia factor.

IQOS Co-Lab Café

Calle de la Horteleza, 87, 28004 Madrid

Metro: Alonso Martínez

Delightful *terraza* café for the summer months, situated in the courtyard of a minor palace in the trendy Chueca district. Open 10 a.m. to midnight.

La Mallorquina

Calle Mayor, 2, 2013 Madrid

Metro: Sol

One of Madrid's most famous patisseries, founded in 1894. It is situated right on the Puerta del Sol, with the bakery counter downstairs and café upstairs where, if you're very lucky, you might get one of the tables looking out over the square. The cakes are unashamedly old fashioned and La Mallorquina is famous for its *ensaimadas* (sweet rolls), chocolate truffles and custard-filled Napolitana pastries.

Hojaldrería
Calle Virgen de los Peligros, 8, 28013 Madrid
Metro: Sevilla
Situated between the Gran Vía and Calle de Alcalá, this patisserie specializes in exquisite sweet and savoury bites in puff pastry (*hojaldre* in Spanish). The Rococo-style interior is as fancy as the pastries.

Chocolatería de San Ginés
Pasadizo de San Ginés, 5, 28013 Madrid
Metro: Sol
One of the most traditional places for late night or early morning *churros con chocolate.* San Ginés is also open at more regular hours during the day for coffee and a selection of cakes and pastries.

Pomme Sucree
Calle del Barquillo, 49, 28004 Madrid
Metro: Chueca
Julio Blanco has been named the best pastry chef in Spain. His amazing creations, from 'the best croissant' to exquisite, intricately layered chocolate fancies can be sampled with excellent coffee at this tiny patisserie in Chueca.

Shops

La Central
Calle del Postigo de San Martín, 8, 28013 Madrid
Metro: Callao
Large bookshop spread over three floors of an imposing and beautifully restored nineteenth-century building, just off the Gran Vía. La Central has a good choice of children's books and foreign-language books, as well as a wide range of fiction and non-fiction, with strong sections on art, photography and design, social studies and philosophy. There is also an airy café on the ground floor and a stylish selection of literary and Madrid-themed gifts, such as mugs, pens, notebooks and bags.

Desperate Literature

Calle de Campomanes, 13, 28013 Madrid
Metro: Ópera
Small, cosy 'international bookshop' with new and second-hand books
in English, French and Spanish. It's like stepping into the study of a
book-mad friend. It probably has the best selection of English-language
books in the city, both literature and factual, with a bias towards arts and
social sciences. The friendly and helpful staff like to write a brief review
for as many of the books as they can, to help you find just the kind of
book you are desperate for at the time. They run a programme of literary
events, plus chess evenings and their popular *Harry Potter* trivia nights.

Tipos Infames

Calle de San Joaquín, 3, 28004 Madrid
Metro: Tribunal
Mixture of a bookshop and café, with a carefully curated collection of
fiction, children's books and non-fiction, mostly Spanish but with a
good selection of English and other foreign-language titles. Around half
of the space is given over to café/wine bar, serving coffee, cakes, tapas,
beers and wines. The space is also used for a variety of literary events,
including readings by invited poets.

Hermanos Fernanz

Calle de Castelló, 5, 28001 Madrid
Metro: Príncipe de Vergara
Unchanging neighbourhood *fábrica*, established for over fifty years,
where the churros, potato crisps and roasted nuts are all made on the
tiny premises. Pick up your freshly made morning churros here or stop
by later in the day for kettle chips (almost) hot out of the oil.

Lavinia

Calle José Ortega y Gasset 16, 28006 Madrid
Metro: Nuñez de Balboa
This modern wine shop has probably the largest array in Madrid of
Spanish wines from every region, plus international selections. It is
possible to try the wine before you buy a bottle, from the in-store

decanting machines. The shop runs wine-tasting events and courses, so you can expand your knowledge of wine types, regional producers and wine and food pairings. There is also a well-rated bar and restaurant upstairs.

Casa Mira

Carrera de San Jerónimo, 30, 28014 Madrid
Metro: Sevilla

Founded in 1855, Casa Mira is the most famous and most traditional place to buy *turrón* (a marzipan-like confectionery) in Madrid. At Casa Mira, the *turrón* is still handmade from the highest-quality ingredients, so it is expensive but arguably the best. The shop also sells delectable glacé fruits, chocolates and traditional pastries such as *Roscón de Reyes*, the cake served at Epiphany.

Turrones Vicens

Calle Mayor, 41, 28013 Madrid
Metro: Sol

Another long-established confectioner (established in 1775) specializing in *turrón*, with a huge range of flavours and different ways to package it up. The store is more modern than Casa Mira, so you can walk around the displays and pick up the selection of *turrón*, in the size of pack that you want. Practical but less atmospheric.

La Violeta

Plaza de Canalejas, 6, 28014 Madrid
Metro: Sevilla

Charming shop selling their original violet-flavoured sweets. These are available in cute little boxes and tins, through to very fancy jars and porcelain receptacles. They make a unique holiday gift – if you don't eat them all yourself.

Man 1924

Calle de Claudio Coello 23, 28110 Madrid

Metro: Serrano

High-quality menswear with a classic style and a modern twist. The designer Carlos Castillo comes from three generations of tailors and pattern makers, with the name of the shop inspired by his grandfather, Ambrosio Navares, who founded the shop in 1924. The clothes are all in luxurious natural fabrics with fascinating textures and patterns in the weave. These are clothes outside of fashion and made to last.

De Flores y Floreros

Calle de Almirante, 16, 28004 Madrid

Metro: Chueca

This strangely named shop, 'Of Flowers and Flowerpots', in fact sells very original ladies' shoes, all designed and made in Spain, in elegant, pretty styles, presented in brightly coloured suede, leather and fabric, with flat or medium-height heels. The shoes are highly rated for their feminine style and, just as importantly, for their comfort.

Franjul

Calle Lope de Vega, 11, 28014 Madrid

Metro: Antón Martín

Women's shoes are handmade to order in this artisan boutique in the Barrio de las Letras. Franjul was established in 1947 and has made shoes for Madrid's high society ever since. There are around one hundred styles to choose from, which can be made in your choice of leather finish and colour. They specialize in vertiginous wedding and evening shoes, with some medium-heel styles – but this is not the place to buy 'walking flats'.

Vintalogy

Calle de Atocha, 10, 28012 Madrid

Metro: Sol

Spain has come late to the trend for vintage fashion and up-cycling, but in Vintalogy, Madrid has one of the classiest second-hand fashion emporia around. Close to the Plaza Mayor, the clothes and accessories are set out over the large floor space of a former textile merchants, so it's a pleasure to wander around the well-sorted and themed clothes, from printed dresses, to jeans, to shirts arranged in a rainbow of colours. The shop has preserved the vintage fittings and signage, with creative displays and shabby-chic armchairs. Also sells furniture, retro homeware and ornaments.

Grassy Jewellers

Gran Vía, 1, 28013 Madrid
Metro: Banco de España
Located in the much-photographed spot where the Gran Vía joins Calle de Alcalá, this classic jewellers specializes in showy high-end jewellery and luxury brand watches. Gossip suggests that this is one of the jewellers where Franco's wife, Carmen, used to go 'shopping' for free. Madrid jewellers struck a pact to share the costs of what she took. The jewellery shop also has a museum of more than five hundred historic clocks, which can be viewed by appointment. This was the private collection of Alejandro Grassy, the founder of the business.

Años Luz

Calle de Alcalá, 111, 28001 Madrid
Metro: Príncipe de Vergara
Super cool, design-led lighting store with an amazing array of light fittings. Most spectacular are the floor lamps which are really sculptural works of art, many by world-leading designers and artists. Step inside to be inspired.

CoCol

Costanilla de San Andrés, 18, 28005 Madrid
Metro: La Latina
Charming craft boutique just off the Plaza de la Paja, CoCol stocks functional and beautiful homewares in muted shades, including handmade ceramics, enamelware, wooden utensils, blown glass, wicker and straw baskets, together with accessories in natural fabrics including hats, scarves and espadrilles.

Julián López

Gran Vía, 27, 28013 Madrid
Metro: Gran Vía; Callao
Wonderful selection of fashion fabrics and soft furnishings, plus all the
trimmings – buttons, threads, fasteners, laces and ribbons. Beautifully
laid out, the shop is a riot of colours and textures. The dressmaking
fabrics are outstanding, with gorgeous printed silks, heavy silk velvet
and soft tweeds.

El Corte Inglés

Calle de Preciados, 3, 28013 Madrid (and in many other locations)
Metro: Sol
The department store of Spain, El Corte Inglés, has branches in all
the main shopping areas of Madrid, with its flagship store in Calle de
Preciados, just off Sol, where it all began. While not the most exciting
shopping, it is useful to know that the one-stop store sells a whole range
of household goods, plus clothes, cosmetics, accessories, books and
personal electronics. Stocks all the standard brands at regular prices,
with stores open throughout the day from 10 a.m. to 10 p.m.

Chronology

865   The Muslim emir Muhammad I orders the construction of a citadel and the fortification of the township of Mayrit, which later became Magerit, before adopting its modern name of Madrid

1083   King Alfonso VI of Castile conquers Madrid during his campaign against Toledo, in the Reconquest of the Iberian Peninsula from the Moorish invaders

1172   Isidro de Merlo y Quintana dies and in 1619 is beatified in Rome, to become the patron saint of Madrid

1222   King Fernando III decrees the bear and strawberry tree as the town's official emblem

1465   King Enrique IV grants Madrid the title of Muy Noble y Muy Leal (Very Noble and Loyal) in gratitude for the city's fidelity to the monarch

1516   The Habsburg dynasty begins, with the Holy Roman Emperor Charles V crowned Carlos I of Spain

1536   Carlos I orders the reconstruction of the Alcázar Palace, which becomes a royal residence

1561   Felipe II moves the court from Toledo to Madrid, establishing the new capital as the epicentre of the Spanish Empire

1616   Felipe III orders the construction of the Plaza Mayor. Designed by Juan Gómez de Mora, it is completed three years later

1618   Felipe III acquires and extends parklands that become Retiro Park

1625   Felipe IV constructs Madrid's fourth wall, which remains in place to the mid-nineteenth century

1700   The Bourbon dynasty ascends the throne. Felipe V is crowned, inheriting the title from Carlos II, the last of the Habsburgs

1714   The Real Academia de la Lengua, or Royal Spanish Academy, is founded

1734   The Alcázar fortress is destroyed in a fire on Christmas Eve. Four years later, building works begin on the new Royal Palace. It is completed in 1764

1759   Carlos III, the 'king-mayor', arrives in Madrid from Naples and initiates a series of urban reforms and the construction of buildings, such as the Real Aduana, the Real Casa de Correos, the Prado Museum, the Royal Botanical Gardens and the Apollo, Cibeles and Neptune fountains. The Puerta de Alcalá is completed in 1778

1798   The new San Antonio de la Florida Hermitage is built, with its impressive Goya frescoes

1808   Madrid revolts against Napoleon's occupying French troops on 2 May, provoking a brutal repression that leads to five hundred deaths

1813   The demolition of highly congested areas, in order to transform them into public squares and roads. The space that currently constitutes Plaza de Oriente is created

1819   The Prado Museum is inaugurated

1854   Demolition begins on the protective walls that limited the city's growth for more than two centuries

1884   Construction work starts on the Bank of Spain, completed in 1891

1898   Madrid inaugurates its first tramline, running form Puerta del Sol to Calle de Serrano

1910   Alfonso XIII strikes a blow with a silver pickaxe to begin work on the Gran Vía, which is officially opened in 1929

1919   Alfonso XIII opens the first Metro line, which runs from Puerta del Sol to Cuatro Caminos

1931   The Second Republic is proclaimed in the Puerta del Sol. Madrid Barajas airport opens

1936   A military coup sparks the Spanish Civil War, which turned Madrid into a besieged city for three years

1939   General Francisco Franco's Nationalist troops occupy Madrid

1974   The M-30 ring road is opened, relieving congestion for Madrid's 500,000 motorists

1975   The death of General Franco brings the restoration of the monarchy under Juan Carlos I

1979   Madrid holds its first democratic municipal elections since the end of the Civil War

1981   Civil Guard Lieutenant-Colonel Antonio Tejero storms parliament in a failed coup attempt

1992   Madrid is named European Capital of Culture. This same year sees the opening of the new Atocha railway station, the Museo Nacional Centro de Arte Reina Sofía, the Museo Thyssen-Bornemisza, the Casa de América and the Juan Carlos I Park

1993   Pope John Paul II consecrates Almudena Cathedral, more than a century after its construction

1997   The Teatro Real is reopened as an opera house after 72 years

2004   Islamist terrorists bomb Atocha train station, killing nearly two hundred people

2007   The Prado Museum inaugurates its new annex

2017   Tourism passes the 9 million mark, making Madrid Spain's top city destination for foreign visitors

References

p. 18: Francisco José Gómez Fernández, *Madrid, una ciudad para un imperio* (Madrid, 2011), p. 17.

p. 18: Mark Williams, *The Story of Spain* (Málaga, 1990), p. 117.

p. 20: Ernest Hemingway, *Death in the Afternoon* (London, 2000), p. 42.

p. 24: Pedro Montoliú, *Madrid villa y corte* (Madrid, 1996), pp. 92–4.

p. 27: Teresa Diaz Diaz, 'Santa María de la Cabeza, única santa nacida en la provincia de Guadalajara', in *El culto a los santos: cofradías, devoción, fiestas y arte* (Madrid, 2008), pp. 637–54.

p. 33: María Isabel Gea Ortigas, *Breve historia de la Plaza Mayor* (Madrid, 2008), p. 20.

p. 51: Fernando Revilla and Rosalía Ramos, *Historia breve de Madrid* (Madrid, 1994), pp. 115–16.

p. 68: José del Corral, *El Madrid de los Borbones* (Madrid, 2005), p. 39.

p. 72: José del Corral, *El Madrid de los Borbones* (Madrid, 2005), p. 33.

p. 85: Mark Williams, *The Story of Spain,*(Málaga, 1990), p. 169.

p. 86: Federico Carlos Sainz de Robles, *Madrid, Crónica y guía de una ciudad impar* (Madrid, 1962), p. 211.

p. 87: Fernando Díaz-Plaja, *Madrid desde casi el cielo* (Madrid, 1987).

p. 94: Elizabeth Nash, *Madrid: A Cultural and Literary History* (Oxford, 2001), p. 54.

p. 95: Williams, *Story of Spain*, p. 169.

p. 97: Pedro Montoliú, *Madrid villa y corte* (Madrid, 1996), p. 229.

p. 100: Ricardo Aroca, *La historia secreta de Madrid* (Madrid, 2013), p. 121.

p. 104: David Mathieson, *Frontline Madrid* (Oxford, 2014), p. 46.

p. 107: *Espacio Fundación Edificio de Telefónica Guide* (Madrid, 2013), pp. 23–5.

p. 108: Paul Preston, *We Saw Spain Die: Foreign Correspondents in the Spanish Civil War* (London, 2008), p. 46.

p. 109: Perico Chicote in conversation with the author in 1973.

p. 110: Geoffrey Cox, *Defence of Madrid* (London, 1937), pp. 66–7.

p. 111: Ibid., p. 79.

p. 111: Helen Grant, diary entry for April 1937, www.spartacus-educational.com, accessed June 2019.

p. 112: Cox, *Defence of Madrid*, p. 220.

p. 113: Antonio Fernández García, *Historia de Madrid* (Madrid, 1993), p. 661.

p. 117: Interview with Ester Uriol, El Corte Inglés, group director of communications.

p. 119: Julen Agirre, *Operation Ogre: The Execution of Admiral Luis Carrero Blanco* (New York, 1975), p. 68.

p. 121: Francisco Umbral, *Madrid 1940* (Barcelona, 2007), p. 201.

p. 124: John Hooper, *The New Spaniards* (London, 2006), p. 401.

p. 128: Ibid., p. 402.

p. 129: Hamilton M. Stapell, *Remaking Madrid* (New York, 2010), p. 125.

p. 129: Enrique Tierno Galván, *Villa de Madrid* (Madrid, 1985), p. 15.

p. 142: Pedro Montoliú, *Madrid villa y corte* (Madrid, 1996), p. 303.

p. 142: *El País* (May 2006), p. 16.

p. 142: *Cinco Días* (January 2017), p. 32.

p. 144: Fidel Revilla and Rosalía Ramos, *Historia breve de Madrid* (Madrid, 2007), pp. 291–2.

p. 146: www.centreforcities.org, 22 September 2016.

p. 163: Benito Pérez Galdós, *Fortunata and Jacinta*, trans. Agnes Moncy Gullón (Atlanta, GA, 1986), vol. III, pp. 433–5.

p. 165: Camilo José Cela, *The Hive*, trans. J. M. Cohen (London, 2001), p. 27.

p. 166: Marcial Guareño, 'Quiere usted tomar un café rico', quoted in Cristian Quimbiulco, 'Diez cosas que no sabías del Café Comercial', *ABC Newspaper*, 28 July 2015.

p. 168: Galdós, *Fortunata and Jacinta*, p. 440.

p. 181: Arturo Barea, *The Forging of a Rebel*, trans. Ilsa Barea (London, 2018), p. 144.

p. 182: Ibid., p. 146.

p. 189: Lorena Muñoz-Alonso, 'Interview with Patrizia Sandretto Re Rebaudengo', https://news.artnet.com, 25 September 2017.

p. 190: Elizabeth Nash, *Madrid: A Cultural and Literary Companion* (Oxford, 2001), p. 106.

p. 191: 'The Meninas Have Become an International Symbol of Madrid', www.madridforyou.es, accessed July 2018.

p. 196: Judah Hettie, 'Interview with Patrizia Sandretto Re Rebaudengo', *Art Quarterly* (Summer 2018), p. 62.

p. 205: Patricia Gosalvez, 'De Lucifer, nada', https://elpais.com, 11 August 2007.

p. 207: Pedro Almodóvar, *The Patty Diphusa Stories and Other Writings* (London, 1992), pp. 90–92.

p. 210: Ibid., p. 92.

p. 211: Gertude Stein, *The Letters of Gertrude Stein and Carl Van Vechten, 1913–1946*, ed. Edward Burns (New York, 2013), p. 228.

p. 216: Elizabeth Nash, *Madrid* (Oxford, 2001), pp. 81–2.

p. 218: Robert Hughes, *Goya* (New York, 2004), p. 130.

Suggested Reading and Viewing

Books about Madrid and set in Madrid

Barea, Arturo, *The Forging of a Rebel* (London, 2018)
> Autobiographical insights on Madrid from Barea's boyhood in the early twentieth century, through to the Civil War.

Beevor, Antony, *The Spanish Civil War* (London, 2003)
> One of the clearest and most readable accounts of this troubled time.

Besas, Peter, *The Written Road to Spain* (Madrid, 1988)
> A history of how foreign writers have viewed Spain on their travels.

Cela, Camilo José, *The Hive* (London, 1992)
> A disillusioned tale of down-at-heel life in Madrid after the Civil War, revolving around a café.

Dunne, Robbie, *Working Class Heroes* (Durrington, 2017)
> The story of El Rayo Vallecano football club, the underdogs of the Madrid football scene.

Epton, Nina, *Madrid* (London, 1964)
> Charming memoir of visiting Madrid as a child before the Civil War and returning in the 1960s.

Hemingway, Ernest, *Death in the Afternoon* (London, 1994)
> Ernest Hemingway's enthusiasm for Madrid ranked only second to his passion for the bullfight, which he never failed to attend when on a visit to the city that is home to the world's second largest ring, after Mexico City. *Death in the Afternoon* is his classic tale of the ceremony and traditions of the bullfight.

Hooper, John, *The New Spaniards* (London, 1995)
> Gets under the skin of the newly democratic Spain and the dramatic changes it experienced in the last quarter of the twentieth century.

Lerner, Ben, *Leaving the Atocha Station* (New York, 2011)
> Lerner's debut novel gives a darkly comic view of Madrid from the perspective of a somewhat-flaky American poet on a foundation grant, who drifts around the city procrastinating instead of writing.

Mathieson, David, *Frontline Madrid* (Oxford, 2014)
Battlefield tours of the Spanish Civil War.

Mendoza, Eduardo, *An Englishman in Madrid* (London, 2014)
Novel set in 1930s Madrid about a hapless English art dealer summoned by an aristocratic family to value a 'priceless' item in their art collection, before the mayhem of the Civil War strikes.

Pérez Galdós, Benito, *Fortunata and Jacinta* (London, 1988)
Social realist novel tracing the fortunes of two women who love the same man: his wife from a wealthy family and his mistress from the poorest quarter of the city. The novel paints a vivid picture of Madrid in the late nineteenth century.

Preston, Paul, *We Saw Spain Die* (London, 2008)
Foreign correspondents and writers in the Spanish Civil War.

Sansom, C. J. *Winter in Madrid* (London, 2006)
A rare English-language novel set in Franco's Spain after the Civil War.

Stapell, Hamilton M., *Remaking Madrid* (New York, 2010)
Culture, politics and identity after Franco.

Stewart, Jules, *Madrid: The History* (London, 2012)
An account of the history and changing character of one of Europe's most fascinating but least understood cities.

—, *Madrid: A Literary Guide for Travellers* (London, 2019)A tour of the great writers who have been inspired by the city, from the sixteenth-century Golden Age, through Romanticism and the poets and philosophers of the Generation of '98, to modern novelists.

Thomas, Hugh, *Madrid: A Traveller's Companion* (London, 1988)
Well-chosen extracts from writers and visitors to Madrid over the centuries which build a vivid portrayal of aspects of the city.

Townson, Nigel, *Spain Transformed* (London, 2010)
A narrative of the sweeping social and cultural changes that characterized the later years of the Franco regime.

Treglown, Jeremy, *Franco's Crypt* (London, 2014)
A masterful investigation into the Franco dictatorship and its victims.

Films

Almodóvar, Pedro, *Women on the Verge of a Nervous Breakdown* (1988)
Almodóvar's commercial breakthrough film centres on Pepa (Carmen Maura) as she tries to track down the boyfriend who has left her, uncovering many of his secrets as she traverses the city, passing by many Madrid landmarks and highlighting the hectic pace of the city in the 1980s.

—, *Live Flesh* (1995)
A complex tangle of relationships between a man sent to prison for crippling a police officer, the police officer and a former junkie who sparks a complicated love triangle.

Bardem, Juan Antonio, *Death of a Cyclist* (1955)
The film explores the consequences of paranoia and guilt when an adulterous couple run over a cyclist but, fearing reprisals, do not stop. Scenes contrast the cyclist's home in a tenement bombed out in the Civil War with the brittle society of the post-war ruling class, the world of the lovers.

Gay, Cesc, *Truman* (2015)
The film gives an outsider's view of Madrid, ignoring major landmarks and focusing on the people, their diversity and constant mobility.

Online

A selection of guides and blogs in English that give an insider's view on what's new, current cultural highlights of Madrid and where to eat, drink and shop.

City Life Madrid: www.citylifemadrid.com
The Local Spain: www.thelocal.es
Naked Madrid: www.nakedmadrid.com
Spotted by Locals – Madrid: www.spottedbylocals.com/madrid/
Time Out Madrid: www.timeout.com/madrid

Acknowledgements

We would like to thank the following people for their help in writing this book:

Duncan McAra, who once again provided his expert literary agent skills. Vivian Constantinopoulos, for her encouragement and guidance in seeing the project through to fruition, and not least, for commissioning the book. We are also grateful to Phoebe Colley, whose editing skills took it through to production. Simon Roth, photographer *sans pareil*, who knew exactly where to point his lens in Madrid. The team at Madrid Destino and the information they made available about the city. José Bárcena at the Café Gijón, who embodies the professionalism of the Madrid waiter. Camino Enriquez at Royal Tapestry Factory, for guiding us through this historic institution. Eduardo Salas, Director of the Museo de San Isidro, a font of knowledge on Madrid's early history. Marcos Seseña, CEO Capas Seseña, for sharing the history of this unique firm. William Faulks, who gave us useful tips about the Madrid football scene. Robbie Dunne, the unrivalled expert on Rayo Vallecano football team. Ester Uriol at El Corte Inglés, an invaluable source of information for understanding the history of this venerable retail establishment. And last but not least, we thank all those we may have omitted, who contributed to our knowledge of Madrid.

Photo Acknowledgements

The author and publishers wish to express their thanks to the below sources of illustrative material and/or permission to reproduce it.

Agencia Efe/Shutterstock: p. 126; photo Manuel Ascanio/Shutterstock. com: p. 15 (top); photo Manuel Pérez Barriopedro: p. 126; Bettmann/ Getty Images: p. 120; Classic Image/Alamy Stock Photo: p. 50; photos Helen Crisp: pp. 9, 11 (top and bottom), 25, 81, 84, 152, 156, 166, 186, 199, 201, 202, 204, 213, 214, 216, 217; courtesy of El Corte Inglés: p. 116; courtesy of El Deseo S.A.: p. 206; photo esp2k/iStock: p. 67; photo Christian Franzen: p. 92; photos fotoVoyager/iStock: pp. 137, 182, 185; photo InkaOne/Shutterstock: p. 15 (bottom); photo Javitouh/ Shutterstock: p. 173; photos JJFarquitectos/istock: pp. 53, 134; photo joeborg/Shutterstock: p. 145; photo juanorihuela/iStock p. 198; photo Paco Junquera/Cover/Getty Images: p. 130; photo kycstudio/iStock: p. 151; photo leezsnow/iStock: p. 138; photo Library of Congress, Washington, DC (Prints and Photographs Division): p. 21; photos Matiaest: pp. 70, 188; photo Medvedkov/iStock: p. 148; photo Günther Müller/Pixabay: p. 40; Museo del Prado, Madrid: pp. 77, 78, 79; Museo Nacional Centro de Arte Reina Sofía, Madrid: p. 164; Museum of Fine Arts, Boston: p. 36; photo Igor Oliyarnik on Unsplash: p. 7; photo Sean Pavone/Shutterstock: p. 14; photo from pxhere.com: p. 170; photo Vienna Reyes on Unsplash: p. 171; photos Simon Roth: pp. 8, 10, 12, 13, 43, 57, 66, 93, 96, 98, 105, 108, 114, 123, 124, 125, 143, 147, 150, 162, 167, 176, 192, 194, 219; photo SergeYatunin/iStock: p. 22; photo Takashi Images/Shutterstock: p. 140; courtesy of Visit Madrid: p. 158; photo Florian Wehde on Unsplash: p. 16.

Jean-Pierre Dalbéra has published the images on pp. 59, 62 online, FouPic has published the image on p. 73 online, Alejandro Ramos has published the images on p. 172 online under conditions imposed by a Creative Commons Attribution Share Alike 2.0 Generic license; Alvesgaspar has published the image on p. 32 online, Barcex has published the image on p. 26 online, Basilio has published the image on p. 29 online under conditions imposed by a Creative Commons

Index